OBEY

Church humor
at
its funniest.

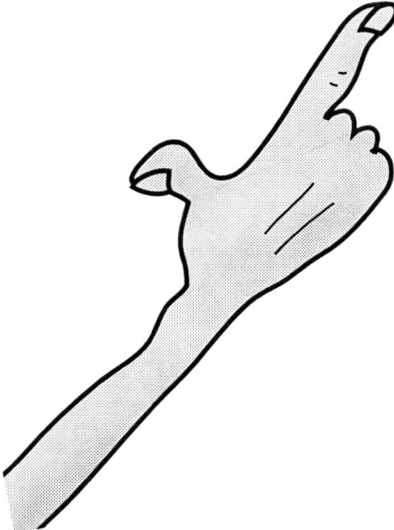

Written and illustrated

by R. Wayne Edwards

OBEY 2nd Edition
Copyright (C) 2006 by FamilyPoet.Com

Cover design by Ron Edwards, BigFeet Creations
www.BigFeetArt.com

ISBN 978-0-9743803-7-7

The photograph on the back cover is of author and his granddaughter, Ella

INTRODUCTION

I thought that a good title for a book of poems about church humor would be *Obey*. The first poems that I wrote were religious humor. When I started looking through my inventory of poems on religion, I found I had an ample supply to fill a book. Of course the first poem in the book has to be my editorial on free verse. It has nothing to do with church humor other than to inform the reader that, horror of horrors, all of the poems in *Obey* rhyme.

There is always a shortage of little quips to add to church bulletins to make them more interesting. I encourage church secretaries to use the poems in this book. I only request that you mention where the poem came from, which, after all, is standard publishing etiquette. My books have become more and more a family project, with every member of the family getting involved. I want to give a special thanks to my oldest son, Ron, who has used his professional skills to design the cover of *Obey*. Of course the family member most dedicated to the project is my wife, Ruth, who has spent more hours then I have, just trying to proof read the tons of stuff that I write.

If for some ungodly reason, you have never read or heard any of my humorous poems, go to the web site that my daughter, Ruthie, designed for me and enjoy hours of reading the one thousand poems and illustrations that I have written on every subject imaginable. When I write religious humor, I sometimes try to include a little moral lesson. Because it is not always readily apparent, I have written an explanation for a lot of the poems in *Obey*. If you are like me, when you read a book that you really enjoy, you always wonder about the person who wrote it, so I have also included little anecdotes of our family history.

You have spent way too much time reading this introduction. Get on to the funny part and enjoy yourself.

R. Wayne Edwards

FREE VERSE

I read a poem
The other day,
It didn't rhyme
To my dismay.

You ask me how
Was one to know
It was a poem?
They told me so.

Scribed in lines
Both crude and terse,
They said that it
Was called free verse.

Why it was verse
Was hard to see
But one could tell
Why it was free.

I read it twice
Lost time I spent.
I still don't know
Just what it meant.

I think that it
Should be a crime
To write a poem
That doesn't rhyme.

Free Verse

I have been including Free Verse in all of my books. It is sort of a one-man crusade on my part to bring rhyming poetry back into popularity. Free Verse has nothing to do with church humor but on the minute chance that this is the first one of my books that you have read, I thought it best to expose you to my philosophy that if a poem doesn't rhyme, how can it be funny?

OBEY

Adam and Eve lived in Paradise,
There was nothing that they couldn't do.
No parents to nag or rooms to keep clean
And of course they had no curfew.

They spent all their time naming critters,
When they weren't too busy at play.
With nothing forbidden to them
A word never learned was "obey."

But God saw that this wasn't good
So he planted a tree by the lake.
"Don't eat of the tree," He told them
"And Eve, stay away from the snake!"

Adam went, "Obey? Yeah Dad, that's cool."
Eve being a woman went, "Why?"
God replied, "Just because I said so
And you must obey or you'll die."

So Adam went off to name things
And Eve went to find the snake.
"A forbidden friend is too cool."
She found him in the tree by the lake.

Births to be painful and heels to be bruised
Were to be our God's awful curse.
But one thing he added, not written in text,
That has surely turned out to be worse.

It was passed down to us through the ages
And it's certainly much truer today.
All the kids with which we'd be blessed
Would have trouble understanding obey.

Obey

The parent's curse that's passed down through the ages, "I hope your kids do you just like you do me!", seems to be one hundred percent infallible. If even God had trouble getting the first children to obey, we shouldn't feel so bad when ours act up. When I wrote *Obey*, a lot of teens were using "went" for "said" and "goes" for "says" so I went with "went." A warning to teenagers; the curse really works, so take care.

ADAM

When God first made man, from the dust and the dirt,
He made him no partner with whom he could flirt.
He made him a garden with critters and plants
But God saw no need to make Adam pants.

He was happy alone, according to story,
As he sat about naming the whole inventory.
With no one to see, he thought it not rude
To stroll through the garden alone in the nude.

And when he had company, it was just his friend God,
Who seemed not to mind, as they talked and they trod.
No clock and no calendar, such a wonderful place,
He never once worried about gender or race.

And, with only one sex, there were none to harass;
Nor did Donkey complain when he called him an ass.
So naming the animals, in God's great creation,
Took all Adam's time, his sole occupation.

His pay was not good but he didn't care,
Thus he became first to live on welfare.
His life was so simple so happy and free,
Everything was for him except that one tree.

So why should he want to mess with his fate?
Why wasn't he stopped 'fore it was too late?
The serpent, I'm sure, had something to do
With Adam discovering that one was too few.

That night when they took their walk in the garden,
Adam took courage and begging God's pardon,
Said, "God, can't you make someone for my sake
With the beauty and grace and the legs of the snake?"

For we read that the snake was a beautiful creature
Who walked up aright and to Adam a teacher.*
"Now things could be better. My life's not a toot;
You know that I have to pick my own fruit."

"You only come evenings to walk when it's cool.
My days get so lonely as I lay by the pool."
Now God was excited and started to plan
A most wondrous partner to help his first man.

And when they next walked, He told of His dream.
Such a wonderful being, they'd make a great team.
Created to serve but with beauty so great,
Not one of God's creatures would have such a mate.

A sweet disposition, a most wondrous soul
Who never would question the first man's control.
Then God made a statement that caused Adam dread.
He couldn't believe what God had just said.

"Just what will it cost for this lovely creature?
Do I need the best model? Do I need every feature?"
Now God set a price recorded in history,
The origin of which is no longer a mystery.

*Gen. 3-1,14

"I can't make a human like a bird from an egg.
This lady will cost you an arm and a leg."
Now Adam, our ancestor, was father to Jew;
He knew that to bargain was what he must do.

So Adam's next question changed history right then,
Considered by some, the original sin.
It caused Women's Suffrage and then Women's Lib.
" God just tell me, what can I get for a rib?"

Adam

Before TV, we had to use our imaginations to supply our own mental pictures while listening to radio programs. There was a program called, *'You Were There'*, in which a modern day reporter covered famous times in history. There was also a program called, *'The Greatest Story ever Told'*, which was a dramatization of popular Bible stories. In *Adam*, I've let my imagination run wild and have given a modern twist to a well-known Bible story. For instance, what did Adam really think about having to give up body parts to have a mate?

HELLUVA SNORE

My daddy was a famous man,
He was well known for his loud snores.
Companies came to test how well
That they had made their soundproof doors.

His snores have caused earthquakes to start
And caused tectonic plates to drift.
And we are sure my Daddy's snores
Had caused the continents to shift.

The night he died, he snored so loud
That he was heard in seven states;
And on his first night up in Heaven
His snores shook all the pearly gates.

Now just how loud my daddy snores
Has fast become an angel's tale;
'Cause after his first night spent there,
The saints packed up and left for Hell.

Helluva Snore

My mom and dad were world class snorers. They could actually rattle glass things sitting around their bedroom. Their nighttime duets would often scare the grandchildren when they came to visit. Every family has its snoring champions, so I am sure that everyone can relate to *Helluva Snore*. Once, while traveling with an inspection team in the Air Force, we carried a combination heavy snorer/heavy sleeper, bed and all, down the hallway and closed him up in the latrine. Of course the rule of snoring always applies. The one who snores the loudest is the first one to fall asleep.

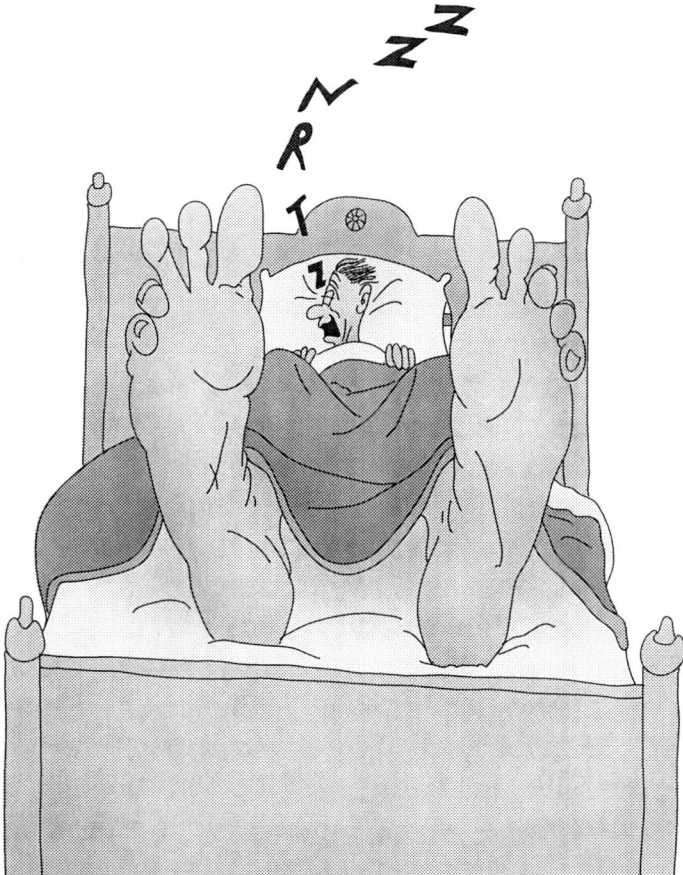

EVE

God made women crafty
But one thing we know about Eve.
When she gave Adam the apple
She had nothing up her sleeve.

I guess I should have put a warning on the cover that this book contains some nudity. I couldn't very well draw Adam and Eve with clothes before they had eaten the apple. Besides, the poem would lose its humor if Eve had on clothes. God gave men the position of authority, but he gave women the talent for manipulation. You notice that the word manipulation starts with man. Webster says the word means, "to manage or control artfully", which Eve did well with a little assistance from the serpent. In all truth, manus is Latin for hand. That is why man is in so many words like "manuscript", "manhandle", "manual", "manage", etc. Eve's God-given talent, for controlling artfully, has been passed down through hundreds of generations of women, along with the truism that behind every successful man is a good woman.

THE COMPLIMENT

The pastor stood by the chapel front door
Shaking hands as the members departed.
An elderly couple stopped to shake hands.
The husband, who was slightly retarded,

Told the preacher, "I'd like for you to know,
Your sermon was really lousy today."
His wife said, "Don't pay him no mind, Preacher.
He just repeats what he hears others say!"

GOD I'M GOOD

So far today God, I've done all right.
I've kept the deal I made last night.
I haven't caused you any pain,
Nor have I used your name in vain.

I haven't thought to cheat or steal.
I think my life has changed for real.
I know you doubt but it is true,
My every thought has been of you.

No gossip from these lips so far,
A better attitude than par.
I haven't argued with my wife,
Nor caused my children any strife.

I haven't said an unkind word,
Or repeated gossip that I've heard.
But God I'm going to need help soon.
I'm still in bed and it's almost noon!

God I'm Good

Ruth and I were married in Tachikawa, a suburb of Tokyo, Japan. Ruth was the daughter of missionaries. We spent our honeymoon with a missionary family, the Bells, in Ikoma, Japan. Reverend John Bell, who lived in San Antonio, Texas, recently passed away. He was one of the early supporters of my endeavors to write poetry. We loved him and his family dearly. He sent me a cute little story about a man who was bragging to God about how good he had been all morning but ended saying, "I'm going to need a lot of help now, God, because I'm going to get out of bed". I had to change it somewhat, I couldn't think of a suitable word to rhyme with now and noon was so easy. You can change the meaning of the title, *God I'm Good*, simply by the inflection of your voice.

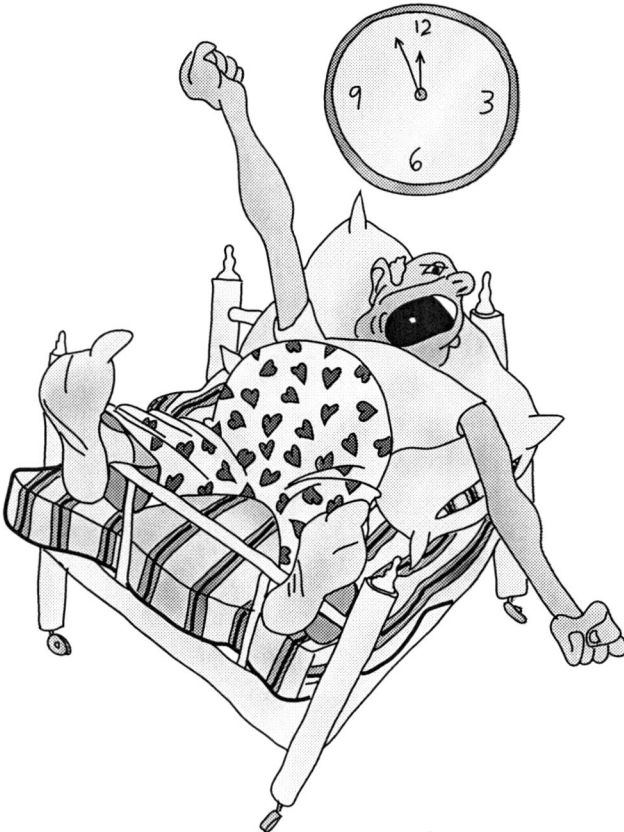

MISTAKEN IDENTITY

It was a fatal mistake
To attempt the mountain pass.
Now he couldn't see the road
Through his icy windshield glass.

Then, when he killed his engine,
Terror filled his stricken heart.
Then his battery went dead
And his engine wouldn't start.

Once he had been a Christian,
So he knew how he should pray.
But would God still hear his prayer?
Would He help him out today?

He had told God in his youth,
That he had no time for prayer.
If he ever needed God,
He would let him know up there.

They found him two days later,
By his truck, down on his knees.
In this kind of a blizzard
Even alcohol would freeze.

Before his God in Heaven,
There's a question he would ask.
"Why didn't you start my truck,
Was it too much of a task?"

God said, "I had a problem.
You know that I'm always fair,
I acted very quickly
When I heard your urgent prayer.

But your voice had changed so much
Since last time you talked to me.
I started another truck
For some guy in Tennessee."

Has it been so long since you talked to God that he might have forgotten how you sound? Praying is easy, but it should still be practiced every day. We recently had the battery go dead in our automobile. We have On-Star, which is supposed to be able to locate us anywhere. It doesn't work when the battery goes dead! We finally called on our cell phone, but they could not locate us, and repeatedly asked for our location until our cell phone battery got weak. The last voice we heard was a tow truck driver in Arizona. That's a long ways from Texas. We finally got a jump from a passing motorist. The poor guy in *Mistaken Identity* sure wished that he had kept in closer touch. Don't make the same mistake in your own relationship with God.

19

BORROWED CHAIRS

The pastor asked the boys to help him
Borrow some of the Baptists' chairs.
They were having their Christmas program
And there wouldn't be enough of theirs.

Their country church was kinda small,
As country churches tend to go.
And when they had a special meeting,
Their crowds would sometimes overflow.

He always took the boys with him
To load the chairs onto his truck.
The Baptist church had no night service
Which he considered his good luck.

The boys complained about this duty,
The chairs were quite a chore to load.
The truck was old and had no heater
And it was a dusty bumpy road.

It was, of course, a two-way trip.
They always had to take them back,
Return them to an upstairs room
And leave them in a real neat stack.

One of the boys said, to the pastor,
As he was carrying one upstairs,
"Why is it pastor, when you don't preach
We always seem to need more chairs?"

Borrowed Chairs

This is one of those put-down stories. The boy wasn't really expecting an answer. He was just getting back at the pastor for all of the work that he was being made to do. We all like to use subterfuge to criticize and then act very innocent with some lame statement like: "I was only asking a question, you just took it the wrong way." Of course, everyone sees through this type of response because they do the same thing themselves.

SERVICE OF THE KING

Pastor Johnson caught up with him
While he was walking down the street.
And he tapped him on the shoulder,
"You're just the man I hoped to meet."

"When you came to church on Christmas,
I saw how much you love to sing.
So I would like to sign you up
To join the service of the King."

But the man assured the preacher
That he was not some raw recruit,
He was in the Father's army
And was an officer to boot.

"But you so seldom come to church,
Except on special holidays.
We could certainly use your voice
In singing songs of Godly praise."

"If you're really in God's army,
Then you must always let it show.
Come to church this coming Sunday
So everybody there will know."

He whispered, "I shouldn't tell you
'Cause it makes some people nervous.
I'm not supposed to come to church
'Cause I'm in God's Secret Service."

Service Of The King

When you read this little poem, see if you qualify for God's Secret Service. There are a multitude of Americans that call themselves Christians who have never seen the inside of a church. The sad thing is that they are bringing up children who will be totally devoid of a Christian background. Very few people, including atheists, want to see the church destroyed. They enjoy the influence that Christianity has on our society. Those who say that they want the Ten Commandments taken off of school walls, still want their children to live by them. The greatest damage being done to the church today is caused by the apathy of Christians.

FHAR DRILL

He was dressed up for the Christmas play,
We all tried not to laugh at him.
He was very much back-woodsy
And all thought he was a little dim.

He was dressed all up in rubber boots,
He had a bucket and an axe.
He said, "Y'all er jus' a laffin'
'Cause y'all ain't studded all the facts."

"I'm one of dem three Bible wise guys
That was foll'ern Jesus' star.
My Sunday school teacher told me
That they wuz a commin' from a fhar."

Fhar Drill

An accent is a hard thing to overcome. It was thought, at one time, that radio and television would cause our language in the United States to become homogeneous but that has proven not to be the case. English contains many words that are hard for some ethnic groups to pronounce. A Japanese, who learns English as an adult, will never be able to pronounce an English R or L properly. Accents are quite often the basis for ridicule and sometimes violence. In the Bible we read in Judges 12:6 that 42,000 people were killed because they pronounced Shibboleth, Sibboleth. In *Fhar Drill*, the consequences were not that serious. The hillbilly's accent merely caused him to wear the wrong costume for the Christmas pageant.

A DOG'S LAMENT

He took a bull and he took a cow.
He took a boar and of course a sow.
He took two dogs and a couple of cats
He even took mice and a pair of rats.
He took grasshoppers and honey bees
But why in the world did Noah take fleas?

A Dog's Lament

Wouldn't it have been nice if we could have personally picked out which animals Noah was to have carried on the Ark? In my case, fire ants would never have made the cut. Scientists are discovering, more and more, that every living creature has a place in the ecology. Even some mosquitoes are pollinators. I think that it would be difficult, however, to sell a dog on the importance of fleas. When I'm working in the garden, there are several other species of bugs that I think we could get along without. In drawing the illustration for *A Dog's Lament*, I indicated who the guilty one might have been that smuggled the fleas on board.

26

TESTIMONY SERVICE

Old Brother Bill is standing up,
About to testify again.
The way he brags about himself,
I know it's got to be a sin.

Sister Smith is getting anxious.
She is going to stand up too.
She'll talk about how hard life is
And what the devil made her do.

Then we'll hear from Sister Lily.
She'll talk about each ache and pain,
About how hard it is to walk
And how she hates to use her cane.

Now Brother Jones is making notes
Of all the wrongs that someone's done.
He's careful not to mention names
But he'll make sure we know which one.

And then of course, lest we forget,
There is pious Brother Herman.
He'll have to let the folks all know
How he hated last week's sermon.

Old Brother Jake finds clever ways
To mention things he has for sale.
Alfalfa hay God's blessed him with
And just how much he gets a bale.

Brother Hank, the politician,
Now he's the one who gets my goat.
He says that he'd get elected
If God was just allowed to vote.

Chose by God to be our sheriff
(At least it's so to hear him tell).
Vote for his no good opponent
And find the fastest way to hell.

Would a sinner seek salvation
After listening to this stuff?
Would he want to be a Christian?
Being a sinner's tough enough.

Preacher's ending testimonies,
Now isn't that just my bad luck.
I really need to testify
Because I need to sell my truck.

Testimony Service

When I was growing up in church, they always had testimony service on Wednesday nights. Quite often some of the older members, women mostly, used the occasion to tell everyone of all of their aches and pains. I remember one poor lady that was very concerned about a soap opera character that was facing a crisis. All in all, it was a good way for everyone to keep the church family abreast of the happenings in his or her life. I never heard anyone advertising items for sale, as this gentleman did but it helped to make a funny story.

END SIGNS

The two priests both stood waving their signs.
Each sign read, "BEWARE THE END IS NEAR!"
Drivers sped by with little notice,
Without a sign of concern or fear.

Then one priest said to the other one,
"They don't notice even when we shout.
Do you think that it would be clearer,
If the signs just read, "THE BRIDGE IS OUT!"?

OPINION

The pastor had been reassigned,
This sermon was to be his last.
He was shaking hands with each one
As the members were filing past.

A little old lady stopped by,
A member that he hardly knew.
She shook his hand as she told him,
"The next one won't be good as you."

"Nonsense," said the young minister,
As he gave her shoulder a pat.
"And just what is it about me
That you'd say something like that?"

"It's like this," she told the pastor,
As the others all walked on past,
"I've been here through five preachers
And each has been worse than the last!"

DEAD CAT

An old man saw a small boy
Looking at a poor dead cat.
It had just been run over
And now it was very flat.

He felt sorry for the boy,
A lad of six or seven,
He said, "Just remember son,
Your cat's with God in Heaven."

The Boy said sarcastically,
"Gramps, don't try to hand me that.
What do you think God would want
With this stupid, old, dead, cat?"

We all assume that children need to be coddled and can't accept reality. Was it Mark Twain who was the first to connect little boys with dead cats? The man in this story injected a little of his own theology into the occasion of the assumed tragedy. The little boy wasn't easily fooled. He didn't think that dead cats had any place in Heaven, besides, it wasn't even his cat.

THE GREATER SIN

The priest had been razzing
The Rabbi once again,
Who believes eating pork
Is a most awful sin.

On their trip to the woods
To look at the fall leaves,
He'd taunted the Rabbi
About what he believes.

We once thought to eat meat
On a Friday was sin
But our church has now learned
Just how foolish we'd been.

I brought ham sandwiches
They're back there in my car.
Just taste one and you'll see
How delicious they are.

The Rabbi now grown tired,
Of how he'd been harried,
Said, " I'll eat my first one
The day you get married!"

CONSIDER THE UNICORN

Let's consider the unicorn;
Each had a horn upon its head.
Have you ever stopped to wonder
Why all the unicorns are dead?

Well, when He built the unicorn,
God made them so that they would last.
An animal, much like a horse,
With legs that were both strong and fast.

With a horn shaped like a dagger,
Unicorn was no mean fighter.
So could anybody's future
Possibly be any brighter?

With such a beauty and a strength,
And speed in which they could exult,
The unicorns were a couple
That had one tiny little fault.

You wouldn't think it all that bad.
It's just they liked to sleep in late,
And this lazy little habit
Became the thing that sealed their fate.

So if you tend to sleep late too,
Just stop a minute and take note.
Because when Noah left in the Ark,
Guess who it was that missed the boat.

Consider the Unicorn

I know that the unicorn is a mythical creature but what if Noah was unable to fit all of the animals, that showed up, into the Ark? Wouldn't it have been, first come, first served? There are certainly Biblical stories where individual shortcomings caused missed opportunities. The parable of the ten virgins comes to mind. We mustn't, like the unicorns in this poem, let our shortcomings cause us to miss out on God's opportunities.

VALUABLE DOG

The pastor was known for sermons
That were too long and uninspired.
It seems that every time he preached,
He very seldom ever tired.

This Sunday had been different,
His sermon had been very short.
He said he had just half his notes
'Cause his dog ate the other part.

A departing guest said, "Pastor,
If your old dog comes up for sale,
I am sure the folks in my church
Would be willing to pay you well!"

SUNDAY SCHOOL TEACHER

"One of the Ten Commandments says
Honor your father and mother.
Is there a commandment that tells
How to treat sister and brother?"

When she asked her Sunday School class.
The first to raise his hand was Will.
Looking at his sister, he said,
"The one that says, 'Thou shall not kill!"

CONSIDER THE SNAKE

Let's give a thought, if you have time,
To treatment of the lowly snake.
Who without benefit of legs
Must travel over land and lake.

He lost his legs, the Good Book says,
Because he tempted Adam's wife
And brought the first recorded fight
Into that happy couple's life.

She'll crush his head, the curse of God,
It says beneath her very heel.
Nor was he given equal space
To tell how low it made him feel.

He says he had a good excuse,
If we'd only listen to it.
He says it was just genetic
And the devil made him do it.

So the snake, down through the ages,
I think received his just dessert.
When he travels on his stomach,
Hot desert sand must really hurt.

Consider the Snake

Have you ever considered the fact, that in the creation story, the serpent lost his legs for being out of sorts with his Creator? It wasn't a small thing that the serpent did. He acted as an agent for the devil to destroy God's perfect plan of creation. Eventually this act caused God to sacrifice His only Son. Up until that time, the serpent must have been well liked. He ran around with Eve and they must have been friends or why would she have trusted him so? He was the only animal, mentioned in the story, that had the gift of speech. When he lost his legs, he lost that ability also. Today, we have just as much to lose when we interfere with God's perfect plan of salvation, as the serpent did. What's more, we are influenced by the same presence that influenced Eve.

ONLY SON

His only son became a Christian
Which was a terrible thing to do,
Especially since old Joseph
Was such a very devout Jew.

So Joseph went to see his friend,
A very strict Hasidic Jew.
"It is funny you should ask," he said,
"My son became a Christian too."

"Let's both go to see the Rabbi,
I'm sure he'll know what we should do."
"It is funny you should ask, he said,
My son became a Christian too."

So the worried Jewish fathers,
Who, all three, thought that this was odd,
Knew that the only thing to do
Was that they all should go ask God.

Just to get this divine meeting
Had been a very awesome task.
When they told God of their problem,
God said, "It's funny that you should ask...."

Only Son

Recently there have been a growing number of Jews that have embraced Christianity. A Jew who accepts the Christian faith usually does so at the risk of losing all family ties and any earthly inheritance. *Only Son* was a humorous story that someone sent me over the internet. I, of course, took the liberty of changing the plot somewhat to make it into a poem.

WIGGLE WORM

Pastor Ben was preaching way too long,
Little Billy had begun to squirm.
He was doing his imitation
Of a giggly wiggly worm.

Billy's mother tried to shush him up,
She shook little Billy by his arm.
She promised awful consequences
And threatened him with bodily harm.

When his sister whispered in his ear,
Little Billy suddenly was still.
Her mother asked what she told Billy
To stop him from acting such a pill.

"I told him if he kept on wiggling
He was gonna confuse Pastor Ben,
And that if he made him lose his place
He'd have to start all over again."

Wiggle Worm

Big sisters always have a way of taking over. My mother used to tell me about how my big sister, Jo Anne, would get me to open cabinet doors at peoples' houses so that she could see inside without getting in trouble. She once talked me into riding down the porch stairs on my tricycle to see if it was possible, and to dance on top of a glass showcase to see how it would look from underneath. She also probably saved my life once or twice, so I still love her. Big sisters often take the role of a second mother to younger siblings.

WAITING ON GOD

Two rowboats rowed up the river
That once had been a city street.
A priest sat high atop his church,
No higher place could he retreat.

"Come down," they yelled, "Get in the boat.
The water's rising and you'll drown!"
The priest said, "God's my protector"
And waved them off with knowing frown.

A rescue barge came to the church.
The flood had reached to the steeple.
The priest said, "God will care for me,
Go and save the other people."

A helicopter dropped a rope
And tried to lure the good priest in.
The priest refused all earthly help.
The floods now reached up to his chin.

The water rose to record height.
The padre sank beneath the tide.
The papers said one life was lost.
The town's lone priest, the one that died.

Now in line at the Pearly Gates,
The priest was quickly ushered in.
God praised him for unselfish work
And for the way he'd hated sin.

But now his faith had failed the test
And so he started to complain,
"Look God, I prayed you'd save my life.
Were all my prayers to you in vain?"

God, quite perturbed, just shook his head,
"You're stubbornness sure made it hard.
I really tried to save your life.
I sent three boats and the National Guard!"

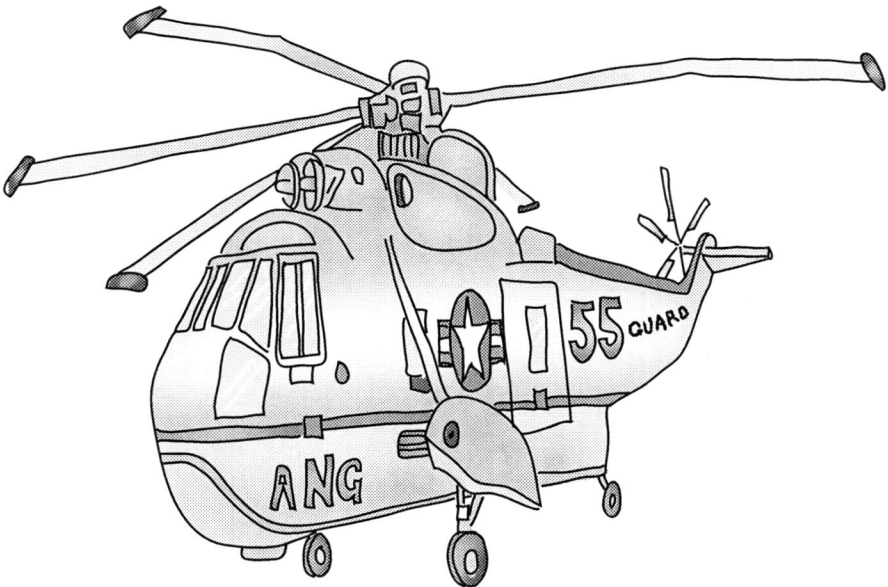

In the twenty-third Psalm, David said, "The Lord is
my shepherd." When using this text for a sermon,
preachers often depict the sheep as too dumb to sur-
vive without a shepherd. Sheep are certainly well
domesticated, and they require a little more attention
than a range steer but they are not helpless. God doesn't
expect us to be helpless either. *Waiting on God* is
about someone who is still waiting on God long after God
has come and gone. If you are waiting for an answer to
a prayer, look around. He may have already answered.

THE ASS'S JAWBONE

When I tell this little tale,
About a man swallowed by a whale,
My tongue gets tangled in what I say,
It won't come out the proper way.

I'll hurry on, I mustn't delly.
Jonah was in the whale of a belly.
Oh dear, not belly I knew I'd fail.
He spent three days in the belly of a whale.

For words like dally I might say delly
But this time I know I'm right about belly.
Jonah swallowed.....Oh leave me alone!
Let's talk about Samson and the ass's jawbone.

The Ass's Jawbone

When we first retired from the Air Force, we went to a small town church with a young pastor named Harry Thrasher. Everyone loved Harry. He preached great sermons. There was only one problem, he made up a lot of his own words. We used to call it Thrasherese. He also had problems with one Bible story, that he liked to use frequently to illustrate some point or another, in a sermon. No matter how hard he tried, "Jonah in the belly of a whale," would always come out as, "Jonah in the whale of a belly." I had a lot of fun at his expense because of it and even made him a little wooden whale with Jonah inside. I wrote *The Ass's Jawbone* with him in mind. He is now the pastor of a large church and is a very successful minister but I bet that he still says, "whale of a belly", when he preaches about Jonah.

A PRAYER FOR RAIN

The preacher said, "Let's pray for rain,"
Because the drought had been severe.
They hadn't even had a sprinkle,
In the whole county, for a year.

The preacher said if they had faith
God would certainly hear their prayer.
"So let's gather at the courthouse
And pray for rain while we are there."

Preacher stood on the courthouse steps
And in a voice both stern and loud,
He said, "Go home, you have no faith.
There's not one umbrella in the crowd!"

A Prayer for Rain

How many times have you prayed for something that you never expected to happen? One especially dry summer, we had been praying for rain almost every service. It suddenly dawned on me that no one really expected God to answer our prayers because not one person had brought an umbrella.

WATERMELON SEEDS

The new preacher had just arrived,
He'd held his very first meeting.
Now a watermelon party,
To give him a Texas greeting.

The two sons of Brother Carter
Were not known for being real nice.
No one noticed them pour whiskey
Over the brand new preacher's slice.

Then they watched and they both giggled,
As Preacher took his first bite.
The look on the new preacher's face
Had been a most rewarding sight.

At last the party was over.
It had been a pleasant greeting.
The deacons gathered together
For their monthly business meeting.

Deacon Jones asked the new preacher,
"Brother Smith, have you any needs?"
He said, "Yes, a little box please,
Because I want to save these seeds!"

Watermelon Seed

Why is it that preachers' kids always seem to be in the center of any mischief that takes place at church? In 1 Samuel, Eli the priest had two sons that caused him a lot of trouble. It was probably the result of being named Hophni and Phinehas. In *Watermelon Seed,* the perpetrators were not the preacher's sons, but maybe Brother Carter was a deacon.

Hobson's Choice

He was a missionary,
He had been one all his life.
How to convince this heathen,
He should only have one wife?

They said he couldn't do it,
The tribe was too ferocious.
Just what they would do to him
Would really be atrocious.

But it was the work of God
So it shouldn't cause him grief.
Then, showing much bravado,
He went up to see the chief.

It really did surprise him
That the head man was quite nice;
And how quickly he agreed
He would follow God's advice.

The warrior chief looked as big
As a hippopotamus.
He had but one condition,
To become monogamous.

And it would test the courage
Of this missionary man.
The chief said, "If you do it,
I will be God's greatest fan."

He told the missionary
How ferocious his men were.
He'd not be responsible
For damages he'd incur.

"See those warriors over there?
They are my five wives' brothers.
You choose which wife I should keep
Then YOU tell all the others!"

CRY BABY

The family was quite large,
The house was always cluttered.
"She's birthed another baby,"
The backwoods husband muttered.

It was this pastor's duty
To visit on occasion.
His wife had accompanied him,
After lots of persuasion.

The old grandma asked them in,
They inquired about the child.
She said, "It's another girl
And my boy is really riled."

"But, if you want to see her,
You'll have to wait 'til she cries,
So just sit, I'll get coffee,
May Beth baked blueberry pies."

Pastor said, "We don't have time,
Even for a piece of pie.
We'd like to see the baby.
Must we wait for her to cry?"

"May Beth went berry picking.
She left me here to mind her.
I forget where I put her
But when she cries we'll find her."

Cry Baby

I've been accused of giving ministers a hard time. I guess that it's because I've been around them all my life. With few exceptions, all of the girls that I dated during my single years were ministers' daughters. I finally ended up marrying one. I have heard many horror stories of occurrences that happened during pastor's visitations. I had an uncle who pastored a church in Kentucky until he was ninety-eight. He told me all kinds of stories involving moonshiners, poachers and other parishioners, of his, that were involved in shady professions.

SHAGGY DOG STORY

Charley had a little cousin
Who would believe most anything.
He believed Charley's frog could fly
And Charley's teddy bear could sing.

Charley would always think up ways
That he could make his cousin cry,
He would tease him and he'd scare him
With almost any kind of lie.

Charley's dad was the new pastor
Of the Methodist church in town.
He was always telling Charley
He shouldn't put his cousin down.

So when Charley's aunt and uncle
Dropped by to visit them one day,
Charley's father laid the law down,
How Charley was supposed to play.

Charley must not scare his cousin
Or tell him any kind of lie.
He mustn't do a single thing
To make his little cousin cry.

The neighbors had a shaggy dog
That was as big as any whale.
Each year they cut his hair real short,
Except for on his neck and tail.

He was a very fearsome sight
And always loved to give you chase.
All he wanted when he caught you
Was just to lick you on your face.

As the kinfolk sat to visit,
In the family living room,
The cousin burst into the house
With a quivering voice of doom.

"There is a lion out in back.
And it has Charley up a tree!
If I hadn't got inside so fast,
It would've surely eaten me!"

Charley's father said right away,
"That sounds like one of Charley's tricks."
So he went, and he got Charley,
And he gave him several licks.

"I sure thought it was a lion",
Charley said through his grimy tears,
"I was the scaredest that I've been
In all my tender little years."

Then Charley's father lost his cool
And with a face a little red,
He grabbed Charley by the collar
And with a voice real stern he said,

"Go to your room and you stay there
For just as long as it will take
For you to convince your Jesus,
That it was really a mistake."

Well Charley didn't stay there long.
It was only a little while.
When he came out his tears were gone
And on his face a boyish smile.

His dad asked, "Did you tell Jesus
How you had lied to me today?
You surely weren't in there too long,
Just what did Jesus have to say?"

"Jesus told me that I was right.
He said that what I said was true
'Cause, when he first saw that old dog,
He thought it was a lion too."

The Shaggy Dog Story

This story doesn't have a moral, unless it is the fact that we all think, or at least hope, that God agrees with our views; when in fact, our views are no more or less important to God than anyone else's. Little Charley is very happy with his way of life and is going to resist any change.   As long as he is successful in making his cousin cry, he is probably not going to stop.

AGE OF ACCOUNTABILITY

In Pastor Johnson's sermon,
He described the fires of hell.
It frightened little Tommy
And he didn't feel so well.

He asked Pastor, after church,
"God knows that I've turned seven.
So how bad can I be now
And still get into Heaven?"

Age of Accountability

This poem asks the question that is very human, not only regarding religion but in our everyday life. Just how far can we push the envelope? I remember wondering, as a very small child, if something that I had done was bad enough to keep me out of the Rapture. Since these are very real concerns of our children, it is important for us to address the issues with them. We must never use religion as a boogeyman to coerce our children into doing something. I once heard a mother say, "It's a wonder that God didn't strike you dead!" That kind of teaching really instills a love for God in a child's heart! I hope that Tommy got a good answer from his pastor. It's just such questions from children that test a preacher's skill.

THE WALL

The great wall, that divides
Heaven from the Devil's Hell,
Was in need of much repair,
As any soul could tell.

Fumes of molten sulfur
Had been seeping through each crack
So God approached the Devil,
At first with godly tact.

"Our wall's gotten shabby,
Bits and pieces lie about.
And if we don't fix it soon,
Your demons will get out!"

"When we repair the wall,
Heaven's angels will do half."
The Devil's only answer
Was his demonic laugh.

God said, "You leave no choice
In the thing I have to do.
So we'll meet again in court,
'Cause I am going to sue!"

The devil's laugh was heard
From Hell to Heaven's foyer.
"Just where in all of Heaven
Will you ever find a lawyer?"

I wrote this poem strictly for its humor. God certainly wouldn't need a lawyer to handle Satan, and it's even possible that there will be a few lawyers in Heaven. They probably won't like it much because no one ever does anything litigious. God and Satan do talk, Job 1:6 lists him as being among the sons of God that present themselves before God on special occasions. There is, however, a great gulf that separates Heaven from Hell, Luke 16:26, so there is no wall to fight over.

ONLY TEN

I lose a lot of sleep
About commandments I can't keep.
I try to do the best I can,
I'm glad he only gave us ten!

What if there were twenty comandments? What if we were still under the Law? The fellow in *Only Ten* lies awake at night worrying that he can't keep up with the ten! If you think about it, the Ten Commandments pretty well cover everything.

PERSPECTIVE

Two little goldfish
Who lived in a bowl.
They thought that their home
Was the universe whole.

"Do you believe in God?",
One fish asked the other.
For neither was taught
By father or mother.

Then answered the son
(Or was it the daughter?),
"Of course there's a God
He changes our water."

This poem is about how two little goldfish perceive the world. Which is, as far as they are concerned, a little round bowl. Our perception of our world must look just as puny to God. I once heard a preacher say that if you put a goldfish, that has been confined to a small bowl all of its life, into a large pond, it will swim around in a small circle, the same size as its bowl had been, for several hours. As a fish farmer, I know that isn't so but it was a good illustration of how we can let our perspective limit our abilities.

65

JESUS SAVES

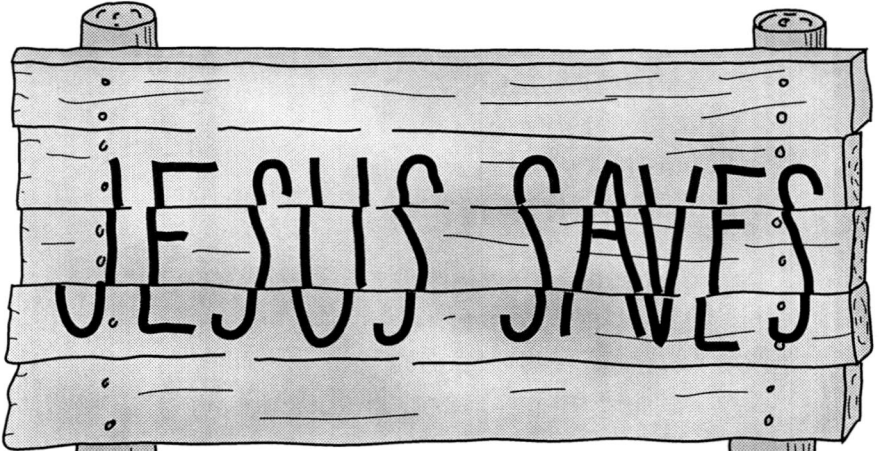

It had been a most terrible day.
The computers in Heaven were down.
The mood of the angels was dreary.
Even Peter was wearing a frown.

The failure had been no mystery,
All the saints knew the cause very well.
It had been a satanic virus
That was sent up from the pits of Hell,

The "Book of Life" had been deleted.
The "Record of Deeds" was history.
To separate the sheep and the goats
Now an unsolvable mystery.

The Devil below was rejoicing,
The chaos he had caused was immense.
No longer restricted by records,
Not one person on Earth stood a chance.

Then came joyous shouting from Heaven
That awakened the saints from their graves.
The records of Heaven were not lost,
Because everyone knows, Jesus saves!

Jesus Saves

Many years ago, in fact many more then I would like to admit, while Ruth and I were living in Tokyo, there was a particular railroad tunnel between Tachikawa and Tokyo that allowed easy access to graffiti artists. The standard, 'Yankee Go Home', had an addendum that said, 'Via Japan Airlines'. On the other side some well-meaning individual had put in big block letters, 'Jesus saves'. It wasn't long before some wag had placed a large metal 'S&H Green Stamp' sign right below it. We all know that God must have a sense of humor just to put up with the human race. I meant nothing sacrilegious when I upgraded that thirty-year old graffiti to the modern computer age.

THE FACE OF GOD

She saw Billy drawing pictures.
He was really concentrating.
He had used a lot of colors
On the work he was creating.

So she asked what he was drawing,
As he drew with an earnest frown.
With the colors he was using,
She thought, a peacock or a clown.

He was deep in concentration
But he acknowledged with a nod.
When she asked what he was drawing;
He said it was the face of God.

So she gave him every teacher's,
I-know-much-more-than-you-do smile,
Looking down upon his desk top,
As she stood watching from the aisle

She said, "No one knows how God looks,
Why don't you draw a pig or cow?"
He said, "No one knew how God looks,
But everybody will know now!"

The Face Of God

Little kids are always impressed with their own artwork; after all, it always goes right into their own art show on mother's refrigerator. In *The Face Of God*, Billy has enlightened the whole world on how God looks. With the exception of George Burns, every portrayal of God, that I have ever seen, has had a long Santa type beard. I guess the beard is supposed to make him look ancient and wise. The teacher was probably nervous about the mention of God in the classroom. If Billy insisted that his portrait was the face of God, then she could not display it in the hallway, along with his classmates' drawings. Perhaps we too could see the face of God, were we to approach Him with the innocence and faith of a little child. Or, as with some religions in the world, Billy could have been told that he could have been executed for drawing a picture of his God, even though his art work was done out of love.

CHURCH

It's my favorite place to be,
Where I can hear the Word of God.
And listen to the preacher tell
Where Bible men have lived and trod.

To hear about commandments ten
And learn by heart the Golden Rule.
To sing the songs that I had learned,
In younger days, in Sunday school.

Old songs that never seem to age
But ever seem to ring anew;
I sing as I stand there aching,
With warm thoughts of my cushioned pew.

As while our learn-ed pastor speaks,
With the words that seem to carry
The elegance that he had learned
In some distant seminary.

And then he always stops to ask,
"Does anybody else feel hot?"
He never sees me shake my head
And mumble that, "Of course I'm not!"

So then I have to wrap up in
My constant friend, my woolen shawl,
And through thick glasses, try to read
Words always printed way too small.

By then my legs have both grown numb
And my whole back, I think's gone dead.
Right then is when I start to wish
That I had stayed at home in bed!

My every thought by then has turned
To all the places that I ache.
That's when I notice, when he prays,
How terribly long it seems to take.

As I obediently stand there,
Literally, it seems for days,
I should appreciate, I know,
His every thought and every phrase.

But the words for which I've waited,
Words I long to hear repeated,
Four little words I never miss
Are the words, "You may be seated."

Church

When I wrote Church, we were attending a church that had a pastor who preached great sermons; it just seemed to take him a long time to get around to them. Quite often, after telling us to stand for a song, he would forget about the song and forget that we were standing! Worst of all, especially for all of us older people, he would forget to tell us we could sit down. The church, like most, had a senior citizen's group, those fifty and older, called *Prime-Timers*. No one over the age of fifty likes to stand when there is a close place to sit down. Seconds seem like minutes and minutes seem like hours. Even though the pastor had a long way to go before he turned fifty, we always invited him to our *Prime-Timers* meetings. He enjoyed the wisdom of his older parishioners, but most of all he enjoyed the good food. We always had potluck and women over fifty really know how to cook. I wrote *Church* and had all of the *Prime-Timers* sign it. We framed it and gave it to the pastor for Christmas. It might just be my imagination but it seemed that after that we always stood a lot longer then we had before!

CHRISTLIKE

Who gets the biggest slice of pizza?
Tom and Fred's argument ongoing.
Mom thought she could fix the argument
With just a bit of mother's knowing.

"Remember Jesus, up in Heaven?
When we argue, He always sees us.
If he were here he'd take the small piece."
Tom said, "Okay Fred, you be Jesus!"

THEY MUST BE WONDERING

She just turned ninety-nine years old
And was healthy as she could be,
So I asked her, as she stood there,
Why all the gloom and misery?

She said that all her life-long friends
Had all already passed away.
I said, "Surely you're not lonely.
You have visitors every day."

She said, "Oh sure, I've got new friends
And I've got older friends as well.
But I know my friends in Heaven
Must all think that I've gone to Hell!"

They Must Be Wondering

This little old lady has her own idea of what Heaven is going to be like. She can just see all of her old friend sitting around up there, crocheting and talking. From past experience, she knew that the conversation usually centered around the one that wasn't there. She just knew that they had all decided, since she hadn't arrived in Heaven yet, that she had probably gone to Hell. And that now they were probably speculating on the possible reasons why; which was the part that she regretted the most.

OUT OF PLACE

Why shouldn't one of them be there,
One of God's most pretty creatures?
I have some of them in my yard,
They are one of its main features.

I told the preacher, right up front,
"No manger scene can be complete
Without one stuck next to the crib,
Right down by Baby Jesus' feet."

The whole committee's mad at me.
I guess 'cause they all voted, "Nay."
But I just up and went ahead
And stuck one out there anyway.

"Now Josiah," the pastor said,
"The committee all voted no.
The manger scene is not the place
For a plastic pink flamingo."

Out of Place

I thought that they were a thing of the past. But the other day, while driving through the small town of Caldwell, where I went to high school, I saw two lawns with pink flamingos. I don't know if it's just a southern thing or if they are making a comeback all over the country. It reminded me of an old redneck story, so I came home and wrote *Out Of Place*. I'm sure Mary and Joseph had a lot more on their minds than putting out a pink flamingo, but there are some who think that it would have added a little class to the scene.

HEROES

He had preached his usual sermon
That the parishioners knew so well.
Not much time spent on Heaven
And too much spent on Hell.

After service everyone
Liked to visit in the hall.
It was there that little Freddie
Saw some plaques up on the wall.

The pastor, noticing his interest,
Ran his hand through Freddie's hair.
"Those people died for others,
That's why their names are listed there."

"Each member killed in service
Has a plaque that's hanging here,"
The pastor said with great emotion,
Barely holding back a tear.

Then Freddie asked a question
That caused the others much delight.
"Which service was it Pastor;
Sunday morning or the one on Sunday night?"

Heroes

Little Freddie had just been exposed to an hour or so of the pastor's preaching, so he was not surprised to hear that people had actually died from similar exposure. He wanted to know which service so that he could avoid them in the future. He had no desire to have his plaque added to the collection. *Heroes* is about boring preachers. My father had an instant remedy; he just went to sleep.

DON'T SEND YOUR KIDS TO
SUNDAY SCHOOL

Don't send your kids to Sunday school
Where they will teach them right from wrong;
Where they will learn to sing church hymns
And learn to worship God in song.

Don't send your kids to Sunday school
To learn the Bible's history;
To learn about the manger scene
And marvel at its mystery.

Don't send your kids to Sunday school
Where they teach them Christian living;
To learn to help someone in need
And to learn the joy of giving.

Don't send your kids to Sunday school
Where children's faith is taught to grow;
Where they're taught to know what's evil
And learn when they should just say, "No."

Don't send your kids to Sunday school
When it gets too tough to make them;
Set the example for your kids
And get out of bed and take them!

Don't Send Your Kids To Sunday School

I heard this as a song long ago. I don't even remember the tune but the message stuck with me. What kind of an impression do we make when we drop the kids off at the church door and head home to read the Sunday newspaper? Three things that families should try to always do together: eat their meals, pray, and go to church. A family that adheres to these three rules will develop strong family ties that will last a lifetime.

STORING UP TREASURES

With so great a wealth, he just couldn't die.
No one can bribe God but he wanted to try.
He'd heard of people making deals with the Devil,
So why not deal on a much higher level?

He knew he was old, he was in bad health.
He had to decide what to do with his wealth.
Well we haven't time for every detail
But he had a plan he was able to sell.

Now everyone thinks that it's just a rumor
But it seems that God has a sense of humor.
He told the old man, in a godly voice,
"Now this is the deal you haven't a choice".

Bring just what you're able to put in a crate,
Not any bigger than four by eight.
Left over money you'll give to the poor
And you'll not have time to make any more.

Now our billionaire, with his usual tricks,
Used all of his money and he bought gold bricks.
They fit real nice in a wooden crate
That measured exactly just four by eight.

It wasn't too long 'til he met his fate
And saw Saint Peter at the heavenly gate.
Saint Peter said, "It's strange, I must say,
A package just came for you yesterday."

"Well, open it up", he said rather loud;
Intending, I'm sure, to draw a large crowd.
God watched from his throne with his godly smile.
Saint Peter just chuckled, "It's road paving tile!"

Storing Up Treasures

I'm sure that God looks at our concept of wealth as something pretty pathetic. Descriptions of the splendors of heaven are written in terms that we, as humans, can only try to comprehend. Trying to describe New York City to an aborigine who has never left the outback would probably be simple compared to describing heaven to modern man. The billionaire must surely have been disappointed to discover that he had taken sand to the beach.

BROTHER-IN-LAW

In a Catholic hospital,
The nun asked how he should be billed.
When he said he had no money,
He could tell that she wasn't thrilled.

She asked if he had any kin.
"I have a sister you could dun,
But she, like you, is a spinster
With no money; she is a nun."

The nun, he saw, got quite upset.
"Don't you know she's not a spinster?
We nuns are married to our God;
That goes as well for your sister."

That thought had not occurred to him.
It was an out he quickly saw.
"If my sister's married to God,
Then just bill my brother-in-law!"

Brother-In-Law

Brother-in-laws always get a bad rap, almost as bad as mother-in-laws get. A man that has a brother-in-law must remember that he is also a brother-in-law him- self. I won't even speculate on the difficulties one might encounter if he had God for a brother-in-law.

THE DEACON'S STORY

Now you asked me to tell you just how I got saved,
What caused me to change the way I behaved.
But first I must tell you that God is no fool.
He knows when you're living by His holy rule.

I was raised up in church and there dedicated;
And when I got sick, with prayer medicated.
My parents believed in the rule we all know,
"Raise up a child in the way he should go".

I won Sunday school prizes from nursery to teen,
In church Christmas pageants, I was in every scene.
And, certainly, I knew each time that I sinned,
For I'd read the Bible from the start to the end.

Then I went off to school and I sowed my wild oats.
I was beginning to leave the sheep for the goats.
"You are so far from home", said the Old Evil Foe,
"You can do what you want and no one will know."

And then I got married and kids came along,
I knew that my life was so terribly wrong.
Church membership was all that I needed
To lead a good life with the devil defeated.

I wanted to pick a church best for me,
Where the people important for business would be.
My life was a lie, what more could I say,
A Christian at church, a sinner at play.

When I went to church and sat in my pew,
I thought them all fooled, if they only knew.
Oh nothing I did was so terribly wrong,
I could pray a good prayer and I knew every song.

The way that I lived couldn't hurt anyone,
They weren't all that bad, the things that I'd done.
For I loved my brother, that's easy to do
But the ugly and smelly, must I love them too?

And I always gave when the offering came 'round.
They collected in bags so coins made no sound.
How much I loved God, you could see from afar.
I had stickers, with sayings, all over my car.

I sat up in front, in my coat and my tie,
Knowing full well that my life was a lie.
Yes I could play church with the best of the best
And then came my chance to put it to test.

They asked me to run in the deacons' election.
I knew that my ruse had reached its perfection.
But then came the question that caused me to doubt;
This simple young child, had he found me out?

From that very moment, right there in my pew,
My whole life was changed, I started anew.
The question so innocent gave me such a jog.
"Sir ...when the rapture takes place,
WILL YOU FEED MY DOG?"

The Deacon's Story

One evening, at our Wednesday night Bible study, we were discussing how a little child might say something in complete innocence that can totally change how one looks at things. After the study, we visited a friend who keeps a week's supply of food and water out for her cat in the event that the rapture would leave it helpless to provide for itself. I recalled that I had the same concern for my caged menagerie when I was a boy. I went home that night, and contrary to popular opinion, I had no one particular in mind, when I wrote *The Deacon's Story*.

PRAYER REQUEST

We church kids all called her Hippo
Because we thought she weighed a ton.
She always sat on the front row
With her bratty unruly son.

He liked to line the hymnals up
And loudly make the sound of trains,
Or take the offering envelopes
And fold them all into airplanes.

When he made Hippo mad enough,
Her neck would always turn bright red.
She'd reach across the mess he'd made
And thump him up side of his head.

One night, while in a revival,
He almost brought the whole church down.
With song book for a hammer,
The brat had just begun to pound.

She jerked him up by his left arm
And then she held him dangling there.
We thought that he'd come unjointed
But Hippo didn't seem to care.

She threw him over her shoulder
And started for the church front door.
We knew next we'd hear the beating,
At least a dozen licks or more.

Well, the preacher stopped his preaching
And the church grew deathly quiet.
Then the little boy did something
That caused a giggling riot.

With eyes round as two big saucers,
And as frightened as he could be,
He yelled over Hippo's shoulder,
"You all had better pray for me?"

Prayer Request

Hippo was a very real woman in a church we once attended. She had two boys and a girl who were soundly thrashed, at least once, during each service. Ruth's mother, who was a missionary in Japan for many years, was teaching a Bible study one Wednesday night when one such thrashing took place. She stopped in the middle of a sentence to say, "I'm glad that you're not my mother". Shortly after that, during our Sunday school class, Hippo asked for suggestions on how to control her temper when disciplining her children. I told her that with our four children, I never gave more then three swats and they stood for "I love you". I told her that she should repeat those three words to herself when she found it necessary to use physical punishment. When we discussed the same topic the next Sunday, she admitted that she had tried, but that it came out, "I love you very, very, very, very, very (and on and on) much." Of course, modern experts tell us that we were all wrong when we swatted our children. My swats were not given to administer pain but to add emphasis to my verbal correction. Such punishment should never be administered in church or in anger. By the way, our four children all turned out great; we have Ruth, an electrical engineer/artist/computer whiz/nurse, Ronald, a professional computer graphics artist/talented singer, Jonathan, a medical doctor/pianist and Timothy, a computer scientist/pianist. The three who have children are great parents as well. My "I love you" swats must not have warped them too badly.

GOD'S FLASH CAMERA

She was standing in the rain,
A smile upon her face.
Her usual fear of thunder
Gone without a trace.

As lightning flashed across the sky,
I told her to come in.
I barely heard her answer
Above the thunder's din.

"I can't come in right now," she said,
"I'm busy as can be.
Don't you see the flashes?
God's taking photographs of me!"

God's Flash Camera

The little girl in God's Flash Camera doesn't have to be a tomboy, but the only alternative would be for her to be very vain. I have a granddaughter who likes to cut up in front of the camera. I imagine that if God were taking her picture, she would act no different. My children were never afraid of thunder but I know of some children for whom it is most terrifying. A preacher friend of ours told his son that it was just God talking and not to be afraid. One day during a very severe thunderstorm the little boy stubbed his toe. He heard God talking outside so he ran and stuck his toe out the door and shouted, "God, don't you know that I hurt my toe?"

FAITH

He was young and he was strong.
He could run the whole day long.
With just the strength of arm and leg,
He could climb the highest crag.

He knew, that with his strength alone,
He could protect both flesh and bone.
So he would climb the highest heights,
Just to enjoy the lofty sights.

One day, with confidence sublime,
He thought that he would make a climb
Nobody else had made before-
A place where eagles feared to soar.

He climbed without piton or rope,
His strength was where he placed his hope.
But then he slipped, with abject terror
He knew he'd made a fateful error.

His strength was useless hanging there,
No way that he could climb on air.
His faith in self began to sway,
At last he thought, "It's time to pray."

A voice from heaven said, "Let go.
Have faith I'll catch you, don't you know?"
But he looked down at naught but space,
His sturdy heart began to race.

No catching hand that he could see.
God said, "Let go, don't you trust me?
You surely know that all you need
Is faith the size of a mustard seed."

Now he who'd made his way alone,
Said with a voice that was more a moan,
"I love you God, and I know you care,
But can I speak to someone else up there?"

How many of us have the faith to 'let go' when God says to let go? I got the idea for Faith from a skit put on by an evangelist who was visiting our church. It is easy to get so self-dependent that we come to believe we don't need anyone, not even God. Then something devastating hits us all at once and because we're not used to allowing God in on our decisions, we don't have the faith to let Him work it out for us. In writing *Faith*, I tried to illustrate just that point. When God says, "Let go", we must be ready to let go. It doesn't take a whale of a lot of faith.

THE BICYCLE

Little Pedro wanted a bike
As bad as any one could want.
All of the other boys had one,
As they were very quick to taunt.

He'd say a prayer to God each day
At his grandmother's little shrine.
"Dear Jesus, won't you just give me
A bicycle that's really mine?"

Once he wrote it in a letter
And gave it to the parish priest.
"Jesus, just why can't you hear me?
Why won't you answer me at least?"

One night he watched a TV show
That made him really stop and think.
Some kids got a lot of money
With just a simple pen and ink.

That's where he got the idea,
He got it off of his TV.
"If it could work for other kids,
It could certainly work for me."

He snuck into his grandma's room,
Took Virgin Mary from her shrine,
And nobody saw him do it
So every thing was working fine.

He hid Mary in his closet
And started writing on a note.
He knew he'd get his bike for sure
Because of what it was he wrote.

"Dear Jesus, I've got your mother.
You know that what I say is true
And if you ever want her back,
Here's what you're gonna have to do...."

I first heard this story at church and it seemed like a good story to put to rhyme. When one tries to make lines rhyme it's often necessary to change words to make them suitable. The plot may have changed but the moral is still the same. Pedro, like so many people today, is willing to stop at nothing to get what he wants from God. In *The Bicycle*, Pedro has applied an earthly solution to try and force Jesus to supply his wants. I doubt that Pedro got his bicycle.

BEAUTIFUL WIFE

His wife was very beautiful;
Perfection in every feature.
"Why did you give me," he asked God,
"Such a very lovely creature?"

God told him, "I am God, I know
The kind of woman you prefer.
I made your wife so beautiful
So you would fall in love with her."

"I have one other question, God.
I love my wife with all my heart.
I get lost in all her beauty,
But, God, I think she's not too smart."

God said, "My plan's infallible,
Knowing the things she'd want too.
If I'd made her any smarter
She never would have married you!"

Beautiful Wife

Our oldest son, Ron, waited for the right woman for thirty seven years before he found Erica. When he was young, he would pray that God would take care of her wherever and whoever she was. Erica probably did the same thing. They both are certain that God was saving them for each other. I had to go all of the way to Japan to find Ruth; or did she go there to find me? This poem is a funny story of how two people were made especially for each other.

HEAVENLY SILENCE

There was silence throughout Heaven,
Predicted in the ancient Book.
And you will find it written there,
If you are told just where to look.

Although this silence was foretold
In ancient Bible history,
What caused the thirty-minute shush
Had always been a mystery.

But now the truth at last is known,
The reason why it did occur.
It happened when I first arrived
And went to where the others were.

I stood in utter silent shock,
As I surveyed the happy crowd.
So many of the ones I knew
Just never should have been allowed.

But it was not my stunned surprise
That silenced Heaven's holy din.
It was the others shocked surprise
When they saw God had let ME in!

Rev. 8:1

Heavenly Silence

If you read Revelation 8:1, you will find where there was total silence in Heaven for about thirty minutes when the seventh seal was opened. Nowhere in the Bible does it explain this period of silence, so I took it upon myself to let everybody know what caused it. Of course, Heavenly Silence would put things a little out of sequence, but I haven't let that stop me in some of my other poems. If you are a Revelation scholar, just read the poem for its humor.

CHURCH HOPPER

We found him on an island
In the middle of the sea.
He said that he had been there
Since July of eighty-three.

He showed us to his dwelling,
He had built up in a tree.
But we saw he'd built two more
So we asked why there were
three.

And he answered, pointing down,
From his lofty treehouse perch.
"Well that building over there
Is the place I go to church."

Then I asked about the third,
Just a run-down little shack,
Sitting way off by itself,
Hidden in the very back.

"Well you can't be happy long
In one church, I guess you know.
That other little building's
The one where I used to go!"

Church Hopper

Everyone knows a church hopper. Every church has one or two. If you speak to one they will tell you that they are looking for the perfect church. Of course if they ever find the perfect church and join it, it will no longer be perfect. I will have to admit, Ruth and I have changed churches frequently. While in the Air Force, we changed almost every two years upon being assigned to new Air Force bases. Now, living out in the country as far as we do, and getting older all the time, we find it necessary to attend a church closer to home. By changing churches, we found one benefit that we had not thought of. We now have a close family of friends in four different towns. We know that the hopper in this poem did not have a falling out with the preacher and he didn't move to a church any closer to home, so he must not have liked some of the church members of which he was the only one. Wonder how many churches he would have had to build before he became satisfied?

GOD IS WATCHING

"Just one apple per student,"
A sign was placed there to say.
It said that God was watching,
"Put only one on your tray."

Then on the cookie table,
A sign penned by the same nun,
"A clean plate earns a cookie,
But you must take only one."

"Take all the cookies you want,"
The words were scrawled down below,
"God's back watching the apples
And nobody else will know."

The Christian mother's threat, "I may not be there to see what you do but God is watching." It worked with me, most of the time. As a teenager I often thought that God must be the greatest peeping tom of all time. Children must be taught that God watches over them as a loving God and not a fault-finding God. He is interested in what's in your thoughts, not in your actions. The little boy in *God is Watching*, doesn't understand this concept at all.

FAITH WITHOUT WORKS

He was an inner city priest
In an inner city parish.
He always had a life long dream,
A dream that anyone would cherish.

He wanted to build a shelter
For the homeless ones on the street;
A place they could sleep in safety
And a warm place for them to eat.

Then one day, while he was praying,
It came to him, the perfect plan.
He'd pray to win the lottery,
So he could help his fellow man.

He told God his lucky number
As he reached up with outstretched hands.
He knew the shelter would be built
And he began to draw the plans.

The many things that he could do
With all those twenty-million bucks.
He'd not only build a shelter
But he could buy some pantry trucks.

Then the day came for the drawing.
He didn't mind the little wait,
Fifty million was a figure
That he could barely contemplate.

But when they called the number out,
The money wasn't his to be.
Big hot tears welled up in his eyes
Until the priest could hardly see.

Next time he prayed a lot harder.
Now surely you'd think God would know,
He just had to have the money
With nowhere else that he could go.

Once again they had the drawing,
His number was not on the list.
But with God his silent partner,
He wondered how he could have missed?

Three times again the poor priest failed.
Did God not love the homeless poor?
Once more the good priest called on God
Lying prostrate on the floor.

"Now God," he said, "It's up to you!
There's nothing more that I can do."
His prayers had been so elegant,
All of the best prayers that he knew.

God you know my lucky number,
All you have to do is pick it.
Then he heard a voice from heaven,
"FIRST YOU'VE GOT TO BUY A TICKET!"

Faith Without Works

The Bible says that faith without works is dead. The moral of the story is pretty clear. If we want to accomplish anything in life, it's up to us to start the ball rolling. If you want to look up the scripture yourself, it's found in James 2:26. Jesus once had the disciples get rent money out of a fish's mouth (Matthew 17:27) but I don't think that he would approve of the lottery.

LAST RITES

"There's a body", yelled the priest,
"Right out on the church front lawn.
It's a jackass someone's dumped
And I want to see it gone."

The sergeant turned the phone call
Over to old Sheriff Gunn.
He could tell the priest was mad
And he thought he'd have some fun.

He said, "I know a dead jackass
Is not among your favorite sights.
But isn't it your priestly duty
To give the dead their last rites?"

The priest, with anger mounting
To the point of mortal sin,
Said, "It's also my priestly duty
To notify the next of kin!"

EXTRAVAGANZA

"It's time to go," the Father said,
As they gathered at the gate.
They've been expecting us for years
And we shouldn't make them wait.

The Son was packed and more than ready
To make the promised trip.
Everything was going perfect
According to the script.

The extravaganza was all planned.
The cast was all made ready.
Expectation filled the air,
The atmosphere was heady.

The Program had been sent ahead
So very long ago.
Every detail written there
For those who planned to go.

The great event, so carefully planned,
Would start on Sunday morn.
When Gabriel, the supporting star,
Would blow his golden horn.

Then Gabriel first expressed his doubt,
Would his trumpet be enough?
With all the fancy shows on Earth,
The competition would be tough.

To overcome those big productions
Would take a Godly act.
"Can we compete with prime time shows?"
He asked with angel's tact.

"It might be best to hold our trip
Until a week from Monday;
A lot of folks will not show up.
You know the Super Bowl is Sunday!"

It is difficult for today's church to compete with the multimillion-dollar extravaganzas put on by the entertainment industry. Some churches try with earthly offerings, such as: people centers, tennis courts, bowling alleys and even swimming pools. The truly successful ones do so with the good old fashioned gospel message. Youth programs are necessary to attract youth but fund-raisers for a skiing trip should not dominate Bible study and worship time. Here, I have posed the question; "How many Christians would be in favor of postponing the Rapture until after the Super Bowl game? While I'm on my soapbox, where did the phrase, "If God tarries, I'll do such and such," come from? My dictionary defines tarry as to linger or loiter. God is not loitering, he knows exactly when he's coming.

CONSCIENCE

They were on the lake ice-fishing
When the church bells began to ring.
They could hear the organ music
And the people begin to sing.

Hank was the first one to mention
Just how badly his conscience hurt.
But they both kept right on fishing.
"Well, my conscience is clear," said Bert.

"You have no excuse for missing,
So I know the guilt you must feel.
I couldn't have gone anyway,
'Cause this morning my wife took ill."

Conscience

Have you ever noticed that the same excuse that will keep you out of church wouldn't even slow you down when it comes to fishing or a football game or shopping or something that you really like to do? Here, two buddies are discussing this very fact. One knows that he has no good excuse for not being in church but the other couldn't have gone anyway because... well read the poem and find out.

WILLY'S BIG RED TRUCK

She was the town's biggest gossip,
No one could avoid her ire.
And telling the village secrets
Was work from which she'd never tire.

Now Willy had a big red truck,
The folks from miles around all knew it.
When Joe's bar needed something fixed,
Willy was the one to do it.

While Willy worked at Joe's one night,
He had a bit of real bad luck.
The village gossip, passing by,
Had chanced to see his big red truck.

She couldn't wait 'til church next day
To talk about what she had seen.
Her angry accusations were,
As usual, on the verge of mean.

Willy just listened while she told
All that his indiscretions meant.
And of the terrible message,
About his morals, that it sent.

That night when Willy parked his truck,
He made sure it was in plain sight.
Right in front of the widow's house
And there he left it parked all night!

CHRISTMAS PRAYER

While saying our prayers at Grandma's house,
My little brother Bobby and me.
We had been to the Christmas tree lot,
Where we had picked out our Christmas tree.

Bobby was saying his prayers real loud,
Things that he wanted St. Nick to bring.
I said, "You don't have to shout so loud
Because Jesus can hear everything."

"I know that Jesus can hear me pray
And so can Santa and all his deer.
I'm praying real loud for what I want
Just to make sure that Grandma can hear."

Christmas Prayer

Bobby wasn't so sure about Santa Claus and he wasn't even positive about Jesus hearing him but he knew that he could count on Grandma. Grandparents, especially grand- mothers, are real pushovers when it comes to their grand- children. Grandchildren are quick to learn just how to manipulate their grandmother; grandfathers are a little more difficult. Bobby was hedging his bets to be sure that everyone that counted knew just what he wanted. When his sister found out his plan, she probably joined in and then the contest began to see who could pray the loudest.

MOUNTAIN

There is something
I want proved.
I have a mountain
I want moved.

A little faith
Is all I need.
Just how big is
A mustard seed?

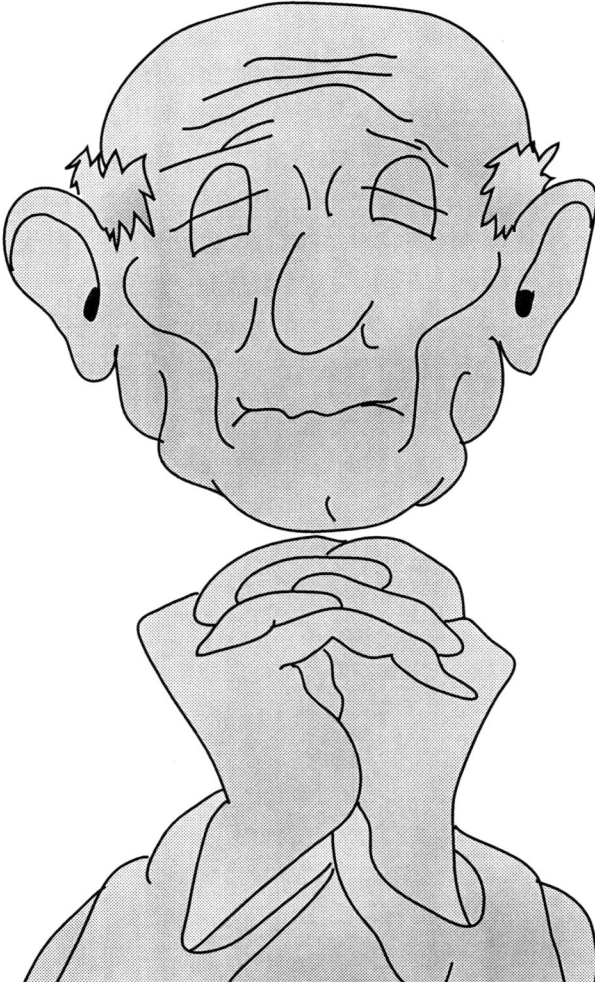

Mountain

Everyone who has ever planted a garden that included mustard greens knows that the seeds are of a pretty good size. They are not the least among seeds that Matthew 13:32 speaks of, nor do they grow into trees that, "The birds of the air come and lodge therein." Some Bible scholars believe that the verse refers to a large herb, Salvadora Persica, that grows in that part of the country and is commonly referred to as the mustard tree. It always bothers me when preachers wax eloquent on some subject about which they know nothing. I recently heard a minister attribute all kinds of ridiculous traits to the eagle, just to bring out points in his sermon. Needless to say, he completely lost me. The same thing with the mustard seed; some ministers go on and on about how miniscule the mustard seed is, saying that you almost have to have a microscope to see it. Evidently they have never seen a mustard seed before. They are about the size of one of the little balls that key chains and light pulls are made of or better still about the size of the small letter o in this paragraph. The whole point of the comparison in the Bible, is that it doesn't take much faith to move obstacles in your life that seem mountainous. The gentleman in *Mountain* has never seen a mustard seed and I suppose he hopes that one is about the size of a coconut, which is the biggest seed in existence.

THE OUT-OF-TUNE CHANDELIER

The preacher said, to the deacon board,
"I would like to buy a chandelier."
The deacons said, "Why waste our money,
There's nobody that could play one here."

One deacon then said, to the pastor,
"You are always asking for the moon,
You know that we are not fancy folks.
Besides, I hear that they're hard to tune."

"Instead of our spending foolishly,
While the church's money is so tight,
We should only buy necessities,
Like the sanctuary needs more light!"

Out-Of-Tune Chandelier

A good supportive deacon's board is truly a blessing to any pastor. There is an English comedy, on The Public Broadcasting Station, which Ruth and I watch, about a woman vicar who has to put up with an overbearing head deacon, who has to put up with an incompetent deacon's board. It's a funny comedy but in a real life situation, the tensions caused by contentious deacons can certainly hinder God's work. I'm not saying that The Out-Of-Tune Chandelier really happened but the story is a good example of why deacons should be carefully chosen. The Pastor, in this case, has two choices; he can let the board know how dumb they are by explaining what a chandelier really is, or he can just go with the flow and let them authorize spending for the new light fixtures that he wants. In the Air Force, I found that the most effective way to get funding for a project, was to let the ones with the purse strings think that it was their idea. It's easy to see the moral of this story. A pastor may sometimes have to use devious means to bring the light to his flock.

A LITTLE BOY'S PRAYER

Lord, I know I have not been good,
And sometimes I've been really bad.
Mommy tells me the things I do
Are sure to make you very sad.

She says that I should pray each night
That I would always be real good.
So if you have some extra time,
Please help me do the things I should.

I know that you are real busy
With lots of things you must get done.
So there's no hurry on my prayer
Because I sure am having fun.

The moral of *A Little Boy's Prayer* is so obvious that it doesn't need an explanation. I prayed the same prayer many times as a boy. "Dear Jesus, help me be good and obey Mother and Daddy", of course I was never serious. We do the same thing as adults, "Dear God, don't let them have those jelly doughnuts at the office again today!"

GOD'S WATER BED

There were lightning flashes
And loud claps of thunder.
It filled little Petey
With both fear and wonder.

Mom said, "Pete, don't worry,
I know it's a fearsome sound
But it's just God moving
His furniture around."

Then it started to rain;
Pete ran to Mom and said,
"Come look, I think that God
Just burst His water bed!"

Just recently there have been deadly demonstrations, held around the world, because a cartoonist drew a caricature of Mohammed. We serve a loving God. Do you realize that I would receive a death sentence for this cartoon depicting God, if I were a Moslem?

MY ANGEL HELPER

Jerry's mother told him
That dark should hold no fear.
"God's given you an angel
And he is always near."

But dark is just for monsters
And Jerry liked the light.
He feared to go out in the dark
And always stayed inside at night.

It was Jerry's nightly job
To shut the barnyard gate.
Today he had forgotten
And it had gotten late.

His mom said, "Don't you worry
'Cause your angel's gone ahead.
He'll see you safely there
And safely back in bed."

So Jerry went out on the porch
And stared into the night.
"If my angel's really out there,
He forgot to take his light."

He yelled, "Angel, I would do it
But it's gotten kinda late.
Since you're already out there
Would you shut the barnyard gate?"

My Angel Helper

A blind person doesn't fear the dark. Other than that segment of our society, a fear of the dark is pretty universal. It's not something that has to be taught to children. On the contrary, children must be trained not to fear the dark. A recent study claims that children's eyes can actually be inhibited from developing properly if parents leave night lights on for them. Not being an expert on eye development, I can only list myself as a doubter. I do know that children who are never exposed to the dark when they are small, have a harder time overcoming this natural inborn fear in later life. In *Angel Helper,* the little boy sees no need for himself and his angel both having to brave the dark, so why not get the angel to shut the gate? Isn't that what angels are for?

JOB

Poor, poor old Job,
He had a wonderful life
With lots of land
And a beautiful wife.

He owned all the cattle
On a hundred hills,
With big barns and houses
And meadows and fields.

Then one beautiful day,
We don't know why,
God went out for a walk
With old Mister Sly.

Now Job was the topic
About which they talked.
And God and the Devil
Made a bet while they walked.

For old Job things went bad
And then they got worse.
His friends all told him
To give God a good curse.

But we know that God won
And Job held the course,
Not knowing that God's bet
Was his troubles' source.

Then God made things better
Then ever before.
Compared to his new life
Job had been quite poor.

Now when things get as bad
As I think they can get.
I wonder if God
Has used me for a bet.

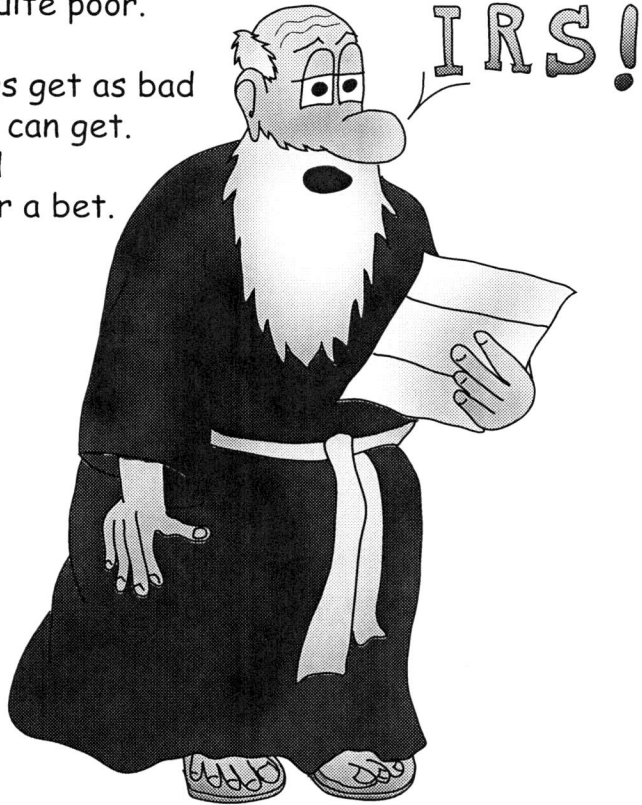

IRS!

Since God is omniscient, it would seem to me that the Devil was the victim of a sucker bet. He must not be too swift. If he has read the Bible, (he quoted scripture to Jesus) then he must know about his certain demise. Why doesn't he just give up and try to plea bargain? It would sure make things a lot more pleasant for us humans. I always thought that Job got a raw deal. Sure, he ended up with double everything that he had before, but who needs two wives? The poem is a tongue-in-cheek poem, and does not reflect the religious convictions of the author, but Job did have one advantage; he didn't have to contend with the IRS on all of his capital gains.

FATAL ATTRACTION

It would be a lawyer's dream
He had rubbed his hands with glee,
Unlimited deep pockets
He would get a princely fee.

The fame of the defendant
Had to make him known worldwide.
It would be the biggest case
That this lawyer ever tried.

His client suffered damages
Unequaled anywhere.
It was a huge temptation.
It should not have been put there.

The defendant, who made it,
Knew of its strange attraction.
No matter how important,
He's responsible for his action.

It's called, "Attractive Nuisance,"
That's what all the law books say.
It means, when you've been stupid,
Someone else will have to pay.

Any jury has to see
It was poorly protected.
There should have been a guard
And a chain link fence erected.

She never would have been there
Had she not been shown the way
By a party of the first part,
On that most regretful day.

No way she could resist it,
Its attraction was too great.
It shouldn't be just her fault,
She had shared it with her mate.

Describing her mental state,
Any jury, to be fair,
Must be told that the woman
Didn't have a thing to wear.

As for any evidence,
It certainly isn't great,
There had been just the apple,
The one Eve already ate.

They found for the defendant,
Though today it might seem odd.
They said the whole fiasco
Was declared an act of God.

Eve was not the only one
That would suffer for all time
'Cause Adam and the serpent
Had failed to report the crime.

De Judge

Fatal Attraction

Ruth says that it will take a lawyer to understand this one but with all of the lawyer programs on TV these days, I think that we all have more legal knowledge than we need. I started to write a long humorous story with the snake as the lawyer but I don't think it's safe to offend snakes. The idea came when I received a notice from Texas Parks and Wildlife explaining a new Texas law on property owner's responsibilities and liabilities. It explained that something like a lake or pond could be declared an attractive nuisance in litigation. This means that even if someone sneaks onto your property and gets hurt, because something you own was an attraction, you can be held responsible and be required to support them for the rest of their lives. Certainly the apple in the Garden of Eden falls under this category. The only thing that saves the defendant God, in this poem, is that it was declared an act of God. Some of us go through life trying to find someone to blame for all of our mistakes. Adam blamed Eve, Eve blamed the snake and I imagine the snake claimed temporary insanity. All they needed was a good lawyer. After all of this explanation, I hope you understand *Fatal Attraction*, Ruth never did!

A WOMAN'S THOUGHTS ON PRAYER

If God answered all our prayers
It might not be too nice.
If he'd answered all my prayers,
I'd have married the wrong man!
TWICE!!!

How many times have you faulted God for not answering your prayers? I'm sure, that if you think back, you can remember times when you fervently prayed for something that you now know, would have caused a major catastrophe in your life had God given you the answer that you thought you wanted at the time. This is one example that I am sure occurs in the lives of many Christians. You could probably add a lot more examples from your own experiences.

POSITION OF TRUST

One day, while reading on the beach,
A lad came up to me.
He asked, "Are you a Christian?
Is that a Bible that I see?"

I said, "I am a Christian.
I read my Bible every day."
He asked, "Before you sleep at night,
Do you always kneel and pray?"

I told him, "Yes, I love God
And I hope that you do too.
But why so many questions
Coming right out of the blue?"

He looked at me and smiled and said,
"I want to go into the water
And I needed someone honest
I can trust to hold my quarter."

Position Of Trust

The little boy has been taught that Christians are honest and can be trusted. Isn't that the way that it ought to be? I have had people tell me that they were hesitant to do business with members of their church because they wanted to avoid possible controversy. Sort of like buying a used car from a family member. If it turns out to be a lemon, what do you do? Christians should do everything in their power to set a good example in business dealings.

ARROGANCE

A scientist, who was of world renown,
Happened to meet God one recent day.
"You know Mr. God," the scientist said,
"Knowledge has come a very long way.

We have to admit that you did it first,
That all living things were made by you,
But we have no need of you any more
'Cause all that you did, we can now do."

Then God, with a smile, knelt down on his knee
And he picked up a hand full of dust.
"With this I made you. If you would be God,
Then creation of life is a must."

"A handful of soil is all that I need,"
Said the scientist then, with a grin,
"The knowledge of man has gotten so great
In a contest, I know we would win."

God just smiled, though the arrogance of man
Was certainly a source of much hurt,
"If you think you can, then create some life,
But first you have to make your own dirt."

Arrogance

Lately there have been rumors that science is on the verge of creating life. When they talk about life, they are referring to chemical reactions that produce microscopic organisms that seem to have some rudimentary similarities to life. When you and I talk about life, we think of dogs and cats. Scientists work in sterile, temperature controlled labs with precise measurements of chemicals that are produced under controlled conditions. All of this is necessary if they are to have any chance of producing (not creating) life. Yet they tell us that billions of years ago, all of this took place in an unsterile primordial soup. I have only one question, "Who made the soup?"

AWK!

A BB GUN FOR CHRISTMAS

I want a BB gun for Christmas.
When Mommy asked me why,
I didn't tell the truth
But I didn't tell a lie.

When I do something bad,
Mommy always seems to know.
When I ask her how, she says,
"A little birdie told me so."

I want a BB gun for Christmas.
Now don't you breathe a word.
The first thing that I'm gonna shoot
Is that rat-fink little bird.

A BB Gun For Christmas

When I was a boy, long before the days of political correctness, the ultimate gift for a boy was a Red Ryder BB gun. When you got your first BB gun, you felt you were ready to take on grizzly bears. After my first day of big game hunting in Houston, Texas, my mother told me that I had shot things that I shouldn't have and took my BB gun away from me for a week. That was one of the longest weeks of my life. When I asked her how she found out, she said that a little bird told her. Actually, I later found out that the little bird was a dead mocking bird, that she found in the back yard. In *A BB Gun For Christmas*, the little boy has vowed revenge on the little snitch. Children should be taught, at an early age, that revenge is never a good thing. Now if you are wondering why I included this poem in my church humor book, read Ecclesiastes 10:20.

CHARACTER JUDGE

I have a knack for judging others,
At that I am the very best.
I can pick the wise among us
And the ones with talent blessed.

My way is sure. It never fails,
For it is simple as can be.
How smart a person is depends
On how much he agrees with me.

Character Judge

This is probably the opinion of more than a few of us who tend to like only those that agree with our point of view. I tend to think that to be a really good character judge, one must be of good character himself. As an Air Force officer, I went to a lot of meetings on a lot of different subjects, quite often with people I didn't even know. It was easy to form an affinity with those who liked my ideas and to be wary of those that didn't.

CHURCH ETIQUETTE

Mama said to us in church,
"You must be quiet as a mouse.
Because you must not forget
That you are in God's own house."

But if it is God's own house,
Doesn't he love girls and boys?
When little kids are happy,
They might make a little noise.

But Sister explained to me
Why we mustn't make a peep.
She said, "Just look around you,
People are trying to sleep."

Church Etiquette

I grew up in church and I know how hard it is to keep quiet. There was a little tree, of some kind, right at the front door of the church. Mother would break off a little switch before every service. She didn't have to use it, just the knowledge of her having it kept me quiet. I imagine that the church custodian wondered why that little tree never did amount to anything. He also probably wondered where the little pieces of limb on the floor came from. All during the service, I would break little pieces off to make sure that it was too short to inflict much pain. Older sisters are great at explaining things to young brothers. Maybe that's why there is so much misinformation in the world. When we were stationed in North Dakota, the Air Force base had a total of about ten trees. Ruthie, our daughter, heard me tell someone that we had so few trees on base that the dogs had to take a number. Later, I heard her explaining it to Ron, who was two years younger than her. She explained that dogs chase cats and cats climb trees. It made perfect sense to her. The big sister in *Church Etiquette* thought that her reasoning made perfect sense too.

IMMEDIATE DEPARTURE

"If you're ready to go to Heaven",
The preacher shouted, "Hold up your hand."
Hank sat with both his hands in his lap.
"All of those ready to go, please stand."

The preacher looking over his flock,
Saw only Hank remained in his seat.
While row by row, all of the others
Were quickly jumping up to their feet.

The preacher tapped Hank on the shoulder.
" If you want to go, I'll tell you how."
"Oh, I want to go", was Hank's reply,
But not if your getting a load up now!"

I remember, as a teenager, hearing the pastor pray
for the soon coming of Jesus. I would think, "Not yet,
I'm not through living yet." Be honest, you probably
did the same thing. In this little poem, Hank wanted
to go to Heaven. He just didn't want to go that night.

CRANKY

That little boy in church,
Ever wonder why he's cranky?
His mom's just cleaned his face
With spit, on a dirty hanky!

Surely, I'm not the only one that remembers those impromptu spit-baths to get off that tiny smudge that somehow was overlooked in your Saturday night bath. It was administered with enough force to remove an entire layer of skin! I still see it administered from time to time, but kids nowadays are much more sophisticated and are as likely as not, to tell their mothers that saliva spreads germs. Anyway, I survived and so did you.

SCAPEGOAT

God said, "Don't eat fruit from that tree
Or you'll surely live to rue it."
When he got caught with the apple,
Adam said Eve made him do it.

Is that why God gave man a wife?
When other options are all gone,
There'll be someone convenient
To blame all of his mistakes on.

God gave Adam a help mate, not a scape goat. In the Jewish ritual, a goat was brought to the door of the tabernacle, where the high priest would lay his hands on it, confessing the sins of the people, and putting the sins on the head of the goat after which the goat was sent off into the wilderness, taking the sins of the people with it.* When God confronted Adam with his sin, Adam was quick to blame it on Eve. Adam, of course, was being truthful as to whose idea it was but it didn't lessen Adam's sin of disobedience. You can never pass your blame off on another, even if it is your wife.

*Lev. 14   144

ADAM AND EVE

When I read about the couple
It becomes quite clear to me
Which one wore the plants
In that first family

FOR BETTER OR WORSE

They had been married for seventy years,
It had been a very good marriage.
It was appropriate that they met their fate
While riding in a horseless carriage.

She had always planned their diet carefully
With just the right vitamins for their health.
Because taking care of their bodies
Was far more important than great wealth.

But now they had passed through Heaven's Gate
And were taking St. Peter's tour.
The wonders they saw were unbelievable.
As written, the gold in the streets was pure.

The marvelous food wasn't fattening,
No need to eat fiber and soybean gruels.
The workshop, the man always wanted,
Contained the most wonderful tools.

He looked down at his young healthy body
And screamed terrible things at his wife.
Something the man had not ever done,
Even once, in his whole married life.

"If you hadn't fed me that health food
With proteins and vitamins galore,
Do you realize we could've been here
At least five or ten years before?"

For Better or Worse

Ruth feeds me so many vitamins and supplements, every day, that I hardly have room for food. I tell her that when it comes time for me to pass on, my body will be in beautiful shape. We all dream of Heaven but we realize that we have too many commitments here on Earth to be willing to let go. Even Christians fight for that last breath and I believe that is the way that God intended it.

JONAH

He tried to run and hide from God,
Somewhere God would never find him,
In a boat to a distant shore
So he wouldn't have to mind Him.

But then, an awful storm blew up
And the crew began to worry.
Jonah knew that he could save them
But that he would have to hurry.

He had them toss him overboard,
Into the stormy churning sea.
He said, "The storm is all my fault
Because God's very mad at me."

But God wasn't through with Jonah,
He had much more for him to do.
He said, "Jonah, you're not finished.
I will tell you when you are through."

God made a great big hungry fish
That had a great big roomy tummy.
The fish took one look at Jonah
And decided he'd be yummy.

Jonah told God he was sorry.
From deep inside his smelly room.
It was dark and cold and clammy
He didn't want it for his tomb.

God gave the fish a belly-ache
And made him upchuck on the shore.
The fish left Jonah lying there,
All covered up with muck and gore!

The lesson God wants you to learn
When you read Jonah and the Whale,
Is that, when God has plans for you,
He isn't going to let you fail.

So never try to hide from God,
When he has things for you to do,
Or he might make another fish
That's big enough to upchuck you!

DISTURBANCE

Her son had been making a fuss
And she was carrying him out.
The preacher, known to be quite loud,
Had just begun to yell and shout.

He stopped and called to the woman,
Seeing her countenance was dim.
"He's not bothering me, Sister."
She said, "No, you're bothering him!"

GOD BLESS YOU

If I meet God,
And I will, if he pleases.
What do I tell Him,
In the event that he sneezes?

Achoooo

A WORD OF THANKS FROM GOD

They all hated the professor
But he had never seemed to care.
He always liked to give exams
But seldom gave time to prepare.

He watched the class with hidden glee,
As they all struggled with his test.
He liked to give them challenges
But this exam had been his best.

When all the tests had been turned in,
Although student comments were few,
One said, "I have a word from God
That He wants me to give to you."

"God said he would like to thank you
For causing such panic, sweat and tears.
Some students He heard from today
Hadn't spoken to Him in years."

GOD'S GETTING BETTER

She sat there on her Grandpa's knee,
As he read to her from her book.
She felt first of his cheek, then hers,
And her face had a puzzled look.

She touched his gnarled weathered hands,
As she sat on his boney knee.
And then she asked him once again,
"And you think God also made me?"

He answered her with grandpa love,
"Yes, Little One, I know it's true."
Then looking at his wrinkled skin,
"And are you sure He made you too?"

Once more she felt both their faces,
As Grandpa said, "Yes, he made me."
She giggled to herself and said,
"God's getting better, isn't he?"

PROPOSITION

Once upon a time, a man,
Although you might think it odd,
Thought that he was sly enough
To actually outwit God.

Now this was the poor man's plan,
How he would go about it.
It is said this story's true
Although I tend to doubt it.

He said, "Dear God is it so,
With you time has no limit?
That a million years, to you,
Is but a godly minute?"

"To me time has no meaning",
Was God's answer to the dunce.
"Time is made for humans so
Things won't happen all at once."

Now, the fool was elated!
God was falling in his trap
And now great untold riches
Would soon fall into his lap!

"God, I know your wealth is great,
And your riches are many
And that a million dollars,
Is much less than a penny."

Now God knew, right from the first,
What the dummy was about.
He said, "Since I made the world,
Of my riches, there's no doubt."

The fool said, "That is great Lord,
Of wealth, I haven't any.
So in strictest godly terms,
Could you spare me a penny?"

God said, "I will be glad to,
To me it is no trouble".
But then what God told him next,
Sure burst the dummy's bubble.

"My wealth, like my love, is free.
To you there is no limit.
So you may have a penny
If you'll just wait a minute!"

Almost everyone who has ever said a prayer, has propositioned God at one time or another. We've said, "God, if you will do such and such, I will do whatever." If God were to hold us to all of those promises, we would be in a lot of trouble (and maybe we are). The man in *Proposition*, has promised nothing in return for the favor he has asked of God. He is probably the kind of person that wouldn't have kept his side of the bargain anyway.

PREDESTINATION

I have a friend who says it's true,
What is to be will be, come what.
He says a man can't change his life,
There is no if, no and, nor but.

I try to think he has some doubt
And that he probably really cares,
But then, I happened to be there
When he fell down a flight of stairs.

Now I know he thinks he's right
Because of what I heard him say.
He said, "I'm glad that's over with."
And then he slowly limped away.

Predestination

When you ask someone if they believe in predestination, it's hard to get a straight answer. Most people will say, "No" and then qualify their answer with buts and how-evers. You can find verses in the Bible to fuel an argument either for or against predestination. Reading Romans 9:11-24 might give those who are against, cause to doubt. I, personally, would hate to think that we are predestined for Heaven or Hell and have no choice in the matter. This story is one that my grandfather used to tell. In his version, the one to fall down the stairs was a minister from a denomination that teaches predestina-tion. It must be nice to know, when you are board-ing an airplane, that you'll be all right unless it's your time to go anyway. But, have you ever wondered what would happen if it were the pilot's time to go?

RESTED

The pastor shook hands at the door.
As usual, Brother Herman
Paused to make his weekly comment,
Critical of the day's sermon.

Pastor knew that Brother Herman
Had never been his greatest fan.
It surprised him when Herman said
That he felt like a brand new man.

He was pleased that others had heard,
Herman's praises did not come cheap.
'Til Herman said it was because
He'd gotten a good hour's sleep!

Rested

Every congregation has one or two people that nod off in church. You come to expect it of some. In our little country church, it was my dad. He could go to sleep standing up. He said that it was because he had faith in the preacher and knew that he wasn't going to preach any false doctrine, so he didn't have to stay awake to keep tabs on him. I was in a service once, when a preacher threw a songbook at a sleeping parishioner. Now Ruth has started complaining that I doze off from time to time. Do you think that it might be hereditary?

ROYAL FLUSH

I wanted to be a circuit preacher
When I finished Bible school.
I never would get rich
But I'd be God's faithful tool.

To build a reputation,
I'd practice preaching on weekends.
I'd taught in lots of churches
And I'd made a lot of friends.

One little country church,
I had liked especially.
I preached there several Sundays
And they thought me family.

One deacon there, a godly man,
I really did appreciate.
And after Sunday services,
The deacon's home is where I ate.

They fixed my favorite food
When they knew that I was coming.
The house was very country
But it did have indoor plumbing.

The bathroom had an old iron tub
On legs like some giant bug.
The ancient toilet was the kind
My Grandpa called a thunder jug.

The nearest neighbor, miles away,
Could hear its every flush.
It made the children giggle
And caused the deacon's wife to blush.

The message came on Tuesday morning,
It really ruined my day.
My deacon friend, the godly man,
Had suddenly passed away.

I had never preached a funeral;
Just the thought had made me nervous
But the deacon's wife had asked
That I perform the service.

The deacon's house was full of people
There was hardly room to walk.
The wife and I had looked around
For a private place to talk.

The bathroom was the only place
Where we could be alone.
The wife sat on the bathtub edge
And I sat on the throne.

We planned a lovely funeral,
Each detail thought with care.
And then we bowed together
And ended with a prayer.

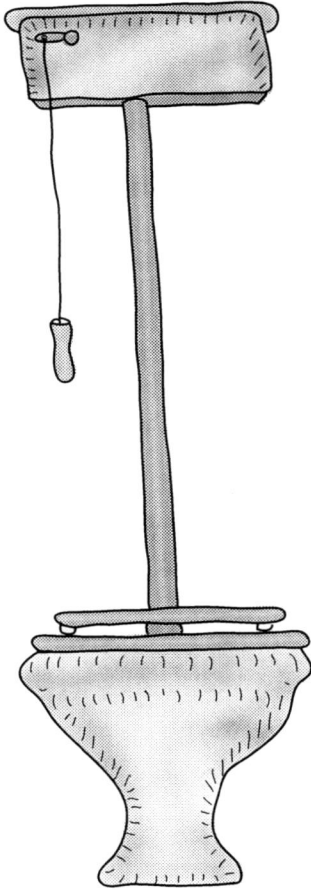

Still deep in blissful reverence,
We both began to stand.
Then from force of habit,
I pulled the handle with my hand.

The talking in the hallway
Became a silent hush.
No matter how you try,
You can't unflush a flush.

This story has been around for some time but it was so funny that I thought it deserved to be put to rhyme and included in this book. The name, *Royal Flush*, is original but the circumstances remain the same. Can't you just picture the deacon's widow trying to explain to the guests that neither one of them had used the toilet while they were locked in the bathroom together? With the event of the e-mail, it might be fun to have people send me the most embarrassing instance in their family's history and put them all together in a book. Fact is always funnier than fiction and I would probably get some good poem ideas. Of course, the names would have to be changed to protect the innocent.

GOOD FRIEND

Sometimes life hands you a rose garden;
Sometimes it's the city dump.
So it's always nice to have a good friend
Just to help you get over the hump.

The *Bible* says a friend is one that sticketh closer than
a brother. Those of us that have no brothers might not
understand just how close that is. The *Bible*, more than
once, tells us just what it takes to be a good friend.
John 15:13 is a good example. I saw a similar drawing
in a book that showed someone getting helped over
a hump and thought that it would make a good poem.

163

SILVER CHALICE

The Old Priest had come to visit,
He was invited for the night.
He had heard about Housekeeper
And she was sure a lovely sight.

The young priest felt the old priest's doubt,
And said to him, "Let's make things clear.
Our relationship's professional;
There is no hanky-panky here."

Then he showed Old Priest a chalice,
Of which he was so justly proud.
He kept it on his closet shelf,
All wrapped up in a purple shroud.

The old priest had been gone a week
When the housekeeper came to say,
That the chalice had been missing
Since the old priest had left that day!

So the young priest wrote a letter
To the Bishop about the theft.
"I am not the type to accuse
But it's been missing since he left."

The old priest responded quickly
"I hid your chalice," Old Priest said,
"You'd have found it in your covers,
If you'd been sleeping in your bed!"

Silver Chalice

The moral of this story has nothing to do with Catholics.
It's about covering up sin. A lie is only temporary relief.
I'm sure that Young Priest had a lot of explaining to do
to Bishop about how he had falsely accused Old Priest.
Do you think that it might have required a few more
cover-up lies? Long, long ago, when I was in college, I
was faced with a similar dilemma. One night I had driven
my old '42 Ford across campus to get a midnight snack.
My mind on the next morning's test, I had absentmind-
edly walked back to the dorm. The next morning, I dis-
covered my car missing and reported it to the campus
police. Shortly after, I remembered where I had left it.
I either had to confess my stupidity to the desk sergeant
or make up some lame lie, like a friend had borrowed it
and brought it back. I wonder what you would have done.

THE TEN COMMANDMENTS
(A letter to God)

The Ten Commandments are changing,
I'm sure it is to Your dismay.
They are not the same commandments
That they were in Moses' day.

Your, "No other Gods before me,"
Is surely not a modern rule.
I am sure that You remember,
We can't mention You in school.

The manger scene and David's Star
Have now been ruled to be taboo.
Darwin's puny explanations
Are what school teachers teach as true.

The world is full of earthly gods
That cost too much to not be first.
And for the God who gave us life,
No longer does all mankind thirst.

Your, "No other gods before me,"
Is in need of a change or two.
The term "gods" must be clarified
By the mighty A C L U.

Your rule that graven images
Are things we should not ever build.
Is a rule that is outdated
And covers way too large a field.

With our kiddy shows and costumes,
We try to start our young off right,
To celebrate the evil one,
The one you call the Prince of Night.

We had to change Commandment Two
In such a way it never fails.
We make no graven images
Unless they, increase our sales.

Now we know that we mustn't take
The name of You, dear God, in vain.
But this limits conversation
And limits what we yell in pain.

We know that curse words always make
The holy name of God less regal.
It's the only way in public,
We can mention you that's legal.

So God, give us a little slack
Because sometimes we tend to blurt.
Add, "It's alright when we're angry
And also times when we get hurt."

Which brings us to the Sabbath Day
And just how holy it must be.
Why can't we show our love for You
Those times we set our ball to tee?

Or out sitting in a bass boat,
On a lake that You've created,
Surely must demonstrate to You
That Your work's appreciated.

So can't we change the words a bit,
So that they're better understood,
To, "We must observe the Sabbath,
Unless the weather has turned good."?

Now we must honor our father
And we must honor our mother.
But it seems that they no longer
Need to honor one another.

'Cause mothers may be several
And change throughout a person's life.
So let's change, "to honor mother",
To read, "to honor Father's wife".

And Father may be anyone,
Somebody we may never see.
So a simple definition
Of the word "father" cannot be.

It is now more complicated,
Though I'm sure it was not your plan,
Now your father may be female
And your mother may be a man.

So we made the rules more simple
And cut out all the fancy frills.
We should only have to honor
The one who pays most of the bills.

"Thou shalt not kill," is way too vague
And right now it needs explaining.
That life does not begins 'til BIRTH,
Should be every student's training.

A woman's choice always comes first.
Sometimes babies are a bother.
And every man that sows wild oats
Shouldn't have to be a father.

You must rewrite the Sixth Commandment,
Give the feminists a gesture.
Thou shalt not kill except within
First, second, or third trimester.

Now Your rule about adultery,
We need to take a look at next,
Because those mighty words of Yours
Must be taken out of contex.

Dumb vows we spoke at weddings,
I'm sure You know we didn't mean,
And You must exclude politicians
And the families of the Queen.

So just add a small disclaimer
So as to make it understood.
"You can't commit adultery
Except to make your karma good".

We can't tolerate the next one.
The one that says we shouldn't steal.
That really sounds a little vague
And makes me think that it's not real.

Should a little creative work,
On last year's income tax return,
Be enough to make one worry
That in Hell's fire he's sure to burn?

So give a little leeway, God.
Make a much better rule by far.
We'll only steal from government,
Or people richer than we are.

Now, "You mustn't bear false witness,"
Is your commandment number nine.
Bet you'd never run for office
When you thought up that little line.

Politics are necessary,
They are what makes our country run.
One has to tell the rotten things
That his no good opponent's done.

So we never bear false witness,
Unless it's just so we can win.
If it elects the man we want.
Then, of course, it won't be a sin.

Number ten, "Thou shalt not covet,"
Is Your very last petition.
Now God, You've got to understand,
It's just simple competition.

When You look down, You surely see
That it is our only basis
To make someone's wealth important
And to separate the races.

Our whole economic system
Would surely go from good to bad
If nobody ever wanted
The things that other people had.

So one commandment we can't fix
But surely you will understand,
When we come knocking on Your gate,
Arriving in Your promised land.

Some know that you created us
And some still have their doubts it's true,
But to be a modern father
There are some things You'll have to do.

The word "command" is way too harsh,
One modern fathers have not used.
Because it hinders self-esteem
And makes your children feel abused.

"THE TEN TENTATIVE SUGGESTIONS,"
Would make us feel so much better
Because we wouldn't be required
To follow each one to the letter.

Now we've made these dumb suggestions,
You know we made them all in jest.
We know You are our creator
And that You know for us what's best.

And those who think you're quick to change,
To meet their ever changing whim,
Make the promise of salvation
So difficult for folks like them.

The Ten Commandments

Have you noticed how different groups of people have tried to reinterpret the Bible, to justify their particular type of sin? My Bible says that we worship a God that never changes. It is pure arrogance, on the part of mankind, to think that they can meet in some upper room and say that God has updated his instructions and such and such is no longer a sin. I read an article in a weekly magazine that said modern Christians would be more comfortable if the Ten Commandments were called the Ten Suggestions. It made me start thinking just how each one could be modernized. *The Ten Commandments, A letter to God,* got a little lengthy. But, after all, there were "ten" commandments and I've included them all. It could be that some of us might have one or two that we would like to see left out!

DISGUISE

She had survived a heart attack
And she was really feeling low.
She prayed to God, "Don't let me die,
I've lots to do before I go."

God said He had heard her prayer
And that He understood her fears.
She had been a faithful worker
So God promised her twelve more years.

Twelve promised years, she'd change her life!
Lippo suction and tummy tuck,
Nose job and a breast enhancement,
Then she got flattened by a truck.

When she met God, she was perplexed.
The things God promised her weren't true.
She asked why God hadn't kept His word.
God said, "I didn't recognize you!"

GOLDEN BELLS

The city mayor had passed away,
The widow asked if I would sing.
I called her on the telephone
To ask what music I should bring.

"He wanted 'Jingle Bells'," she said,
As she was fighting back her tears.
I thought it strange, but well I knew,
The mayor had gotten up in years.

So, next day at the funeral,
In my most solemn reverent voice,
I sang "Jingle Bells", three verses,
Although I thought it a strange choice.

I got a lot of real odd looks
And folks all sort of shied away
But I had sung the mayor's request
And knowing that had made my day.

The widow stopped me as I left,
She told me old age really tells.
The song the mayor asked that I sing,
Was, "When They Ring Those Golden Bells."

Golden Bells

I heard this story on the radio. I don't know if it really happened to someone but I could just imagine how embarrassing it would be to sing Jingle Bells at a friend's funeral, especially if it wasn't Christmas. One thing that makes a funny story is someone's pain. Another thing is someone's embarrassment.

NEW DRESS

His wife went shopping at the Mall
So very much to his distress.
He said, "You can look but don't buy,
You sure don't need another dress."

But then she found the perfect gown,
It cost too much and she knew it.
So when her husband asked her why,
She said the Devil made her do it.

Say, "Get thee behind me Satan"
It's just willpower that you lack.
"I did, that's when Satan told me,
'WOW, you should see it from the back!"

GOD'S DOLLAR

Two crispy new one-dollar bills,
Mother gave to little Andy.
One bill to give in Sunday school
And one bill to spend on candy.

Although it was bright and sunny,
It was a very windy day.
A gust of wind just came along
And snatched both of the bills away.

One bill stuck on a chain-link fence
And Andy grabbed it just in time.
He said, "God, when you grabbed your bill
You just about made me lose mine."

A LITTLE GIRL'S JONAH STORY

Teacher said the Jonah fable
Was nothing but a story tale.
She said a man could never fit
Through the narrow throat of a whale.

Peggy said, "It's in the Bible
And so the story must be true.
Do you think God, who made the whale,
Doesn't know what a whale can do?"

Teacher said, "That's just foolishness,
If you believe it, I don't care!"
Peggy said, "Jonah's in Heaven
I will ask him when I get there.

"He might not have gone to Heaven,
What if your Jonah went to Hell?"
"Well teacher, if you think he's there,
You can ask him about the whale!"

DEAD CHURCH

The pastor called 911,
He didn't know what to do.
A member had died in church,
Sitting right there in his pew!

When the EMT got there,
They called 911 and said,
They'd carried four members out
Before they found which one was dead!

BINGO PRAYER

Their boat was beginning to sink
And it was time for them to pray.
But neither one of them knew how;
Neither one knew just what to say.

One of them lived next to a church,
He said that he had heard them pray.
He said he would give it a try
And maybe they would be okay.

He prayed the prayer that he had heard;
B-9, I-20, N-32.
Then the two of them just sat there
Waiting to see what God would do.

FEARLESS

The Devil went to church one day
To have a little Devil fun.
He threatened all the people there
Just to see how fast they'd run.

The church cleared out in record time,
Except for Pete who didn't budge.
"One in fifty," the Devil thought,
But even one soul he'd begrudge.

He asked Pete why he wasn't scared.
Pete said, "God shields me from all fears.
And besides, I know your sister,
I've been married to her for years!"

RIDDLE

Adam, God made out of dust.
To make me first, he thought he must.
So I was made before the man,
To answer God's most holy plan.

A living being I became
And Adam gave to me a name.
I from his presence then withdrew
And more of Adam never knew.

I did my maker's law obey,
Nor ever once from it did stray.
Around the globe I go in fear
But seldom on the earth appear.

For plans that only God did see,
He put a living soul in me.
Though I was free of any sin,
He took the soul from me again.

And when from me the soul did flee,
I was again as God made me.
My brothers walk beneath the sun
But no legs have I with which to run.

So without hands or feet or soul,
I travel far from pole to pole.
And many people, young and old,
By my death did light behold.

No right or wrong can I conceive,
Nor can the scriptures I believe.
Although my name is therein found,
They are to me an empty sound.

No fear of death doth trouble me.
Real happiness I'll never see.
To Heaven I shall never go
Nor to Hell so far below.

So search your Bible if you care.
Four times my name is mentioned there.
King James, the version you must use.
The other ones would just confuse.

I'm going to end with a riddle. It's an old riddle that has been circulating around for a long time. Some of the hints may be a little dated, so keep that in mind as you try to solve it. I rewrote it and I changed the rhythm to match my particular style. I imagine that the person who originated the riddle has long ago departed this world. One particular hint would date it sometime in the 1800's. Don't be too quick to look for the answer but if you must give up, it is included somewhere in The *Shaggy Dog Story* on page 52. You can cross check your answer by looking for the same word in the introductions to *Faith* on page 91 or *Ass's Jawbone* on page 43. If you really get desperate, read *Jonah* on page 148.

INDEX

BOOKS BY THE AUTHOR

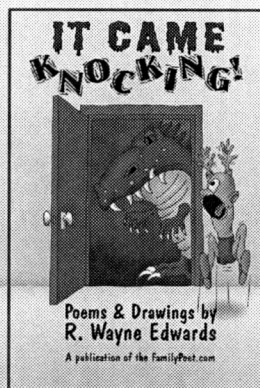

IT CAME KNOCKING!
Poems & Drawings by
R. Wayne Edwards
A publication of the FamilyPoet.com

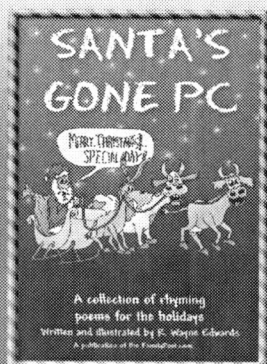

SANTA'S GONE PC
MERRY CHRISTMAS SPECIAL DAY!
A collection of rhyming poems for the holidays
Written and illustrated by R. Wayne Edwards
A publication of the FamilyPoet.com

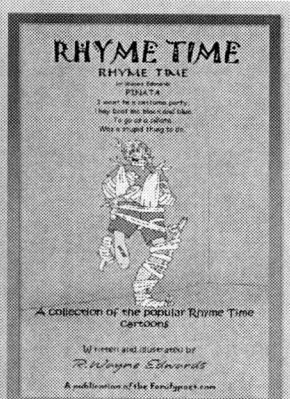

RHYME TIME
A collection of the popular Rhyme Time Cartoons
Written and illustrated by
R. Wayne Edwards
A publication of the FamilyPoet.com

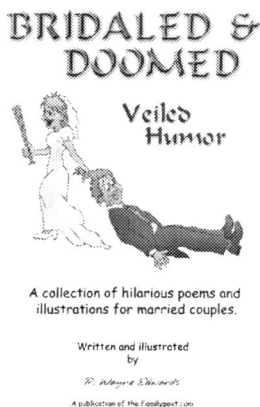

BRIDALED & DOOMED
Veiled Humor
A collection of hilarious poems and illustrations for married couples.
Written and illustrated by
R. Wayne Edwards
A publication of the FamilyPoet.com

The Fork
A collection of rhyming poems of inspiration for Christians
Written and Illustrated by
R. Wayne Edwards
A publication of the FamilyPoet.com

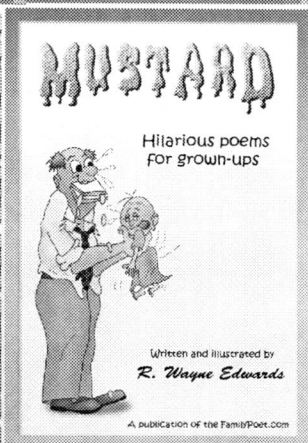

MUSTARD
Hilarious poems for grown-ups
Written and illustrated by
R. Wayne Edwards
A publication of the FamilyPoet.com

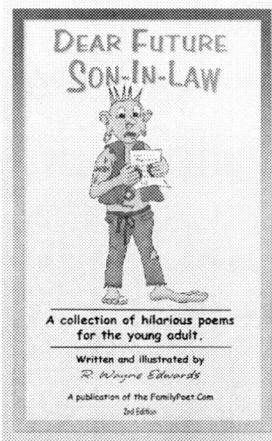

DEAR FUTURE SON-IN-LAW
A collection of hilarious poems for the young adult.
Written and illustrated by
R. Wayne Edwards
A publication of the FamilyPoet.Com
2nd Edition

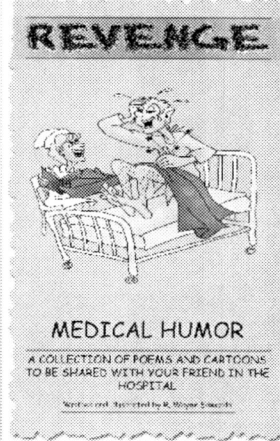

REVENGE
MEDICAL HUMOR
A COLLECTION OF POEMS AND CARTOONS TO BE SHARED WITH YOUR FRIEND IN THE HOSPITAL
Written and illustrated by R. Wayne Edwards

YOUTHFUL REFLECTIONS
A selection of humorous poems about growing old gracefully.
Written and illustrated by R. Wayne Edwards

Printed in the United States
69183LVS00002B/367-414